I didn't see it coming

I didn't see it c●ming

The Only Book You'll Ever Need to Avoid Being Blindsided in Business

NANCY C.
WIDMANN

ELAINE J.
EISENMAN, PhD

AMY DORN
KOPELAN

BICENTENNIAL
1807
WILEY
2007
BICENTENNIAL

John Wiley & Sons, Inc.

Published by John Wiley & Sons, Inc., Hoboken, New Jersey.
Published simultaneously in Canada.

Wiley Bicentennial Logo: Richard J. Pacifico

For general information on our other products and services or for technical support, please contact our Customer Care Department within the United States at (800) 762-2974, outside the United States at (317) 572-3993 or fax (317) 572-4002.

Wiley also publishes its books in a variety of electronic formats. Some content that appears in print may not be available in electronic books. For more information about Wiley products, visit our web site at www.wiley.com.

Library of Congress Cataloging-in-Publication Data:

Widmann, Nancy C., 1942–
    I didn't see it coming : the only book you'll ever need to avoid being blindsided in business / Nancy C. Widmann, Elaine J. Eisenman, and Amy Dorn Kopelan.
        p.   cm.
    Includes bibliographical references.
    ISBN 978-0-470-11645-6 (cloth)
    1. Leadership.   2. Management.   3. Work environment.   4. Success in business—Psychological aspects.   I. Eisenman, Elaine J., 1948–.
II. Kopelan, Amy Dorn, 1951–.   III. Title.
HD57.7.W53   2007
658.4'09—dc22

                                                                        2006036664

Printed in the United States of America.

10   9   8   7   6   5   4   3   2   1

From Nancy: To my mother Eileen, who taught me to laugh.

To my sister Jane, who never fails to show me incredible loyalty and courage.

To my daughter Sabina, who brings love to my life, the greatest gift of all.

From Elaine: To Steven, the love of my life, mentor and muse, for always being there for me.

To Jessica, Peter, and Matthew, for bringing me unbounded joy, love, constant challenge, high levels of absurdity, and new perspectives.

To Lea and Sam Scott, for their constant support and encouragement.

From Amy: To my husband Rik, whose vision and strength constantly inspire me.

To my three sons, Brett, Adam, and Taylor, for their support, imagination, and love.

CONTENTS

Contents

Acknowledgments

The 10 Top Reasons This Book Is in Your Hands

J im Levine, the best in the business, a literary agent extraordinaire who managed this book with amazing tenacity and grace. His integrity and insight are simply unparalleled.

Armin Brott, a talented writer who "got it" and helped us to polish our words and pull it all together—a man of delightful humor and patience.

Emily Conway, an insightful and supportive editor and important member of our team who shared our vision. Her advocacy and enthusiasm were critical; she listens to her authors' voices and encourages them to take chances.

Many clients and colleagues, wise men and women who shared their insights, experiences, and perspectives. Their candor added so much to the value of this book; their honesty and openness brought wisdom and sensibility, allowing us to make sense of it all.

Friends and family, the most dedicated, patient, and encouraging group of people who stuck with us at every turn through the long journey and never stopped believing in us and in the book.

Three remarkable bosses: Peter Lund, former CEO, CBS Inc.; Dan Burke, former COO, Capital Cities/ABC Inc.; and Dan Gross, former CEO of Enhance Financial Services Group, all remarkable leaders in their industries. Peter Lund encouraged Nancy to take on challenges and reach for the top. Dan Burke supported Amy's creative and entrepreneurial thinking. Dan Gross showed Elaine why always considering the next possibility would allow her to take important risks

Jeanette Sarkisian Wagner, vice chair emerita, The Estee Lauder Companies, role model and sage, who showed Amy how women lead with strength, compassion, and a standard of excellence.

Sir Howard Stringer and John A. Lack, bosses and mentors for Nancy at CBS. Sir Howard set a leadership standard with a unique combination of genius, charm, and humanity; John created the template for style and substance.

Jill Kanin Lovers, board member extraordinaire; Victoria Berger Gross, senior vice president at Tiffany & Co.; and Susan Stautberg, CEO of PartnerCom and founder of the Belizean Grove, for always providing Elaine a sounding board and a reality check.

Cleo, a devoted friend who spent countless hours listening to our words, our edits, our debates, and never lost faith.

INTRODUCTION

Over the past 10 years, the business world has undergone an extraordinary transformation. Thousands of talented corporate soldiers who had successfully synergized, partnered, teamed up, downsized, restructured, realigned, cut costs, cut salaries, inflated profits, combined jobs, fired employees, and done everything to make it work suddenly found themselves out of a job. Their companies merged or self-destructed, or a consultant came in, or a new boss—and out went the same leaders who had been yesterday's heroes.

It didn't have to happen—or at least it didn't have to come as so much of a surprise. A lot of these executives would still be at their old jobs if they had paid closer attention to the corporate land mines in their path, to the subtle or not-so-subtle warning signs that trouble was brewing, to the risky political scenarios and the relationship perils that ultimately destroyed or derailed them. But they didn't. And they got blindsided.

SO WHO ARE WE?

Our backgrounds are from both inside and outside the organization. Among the three of us, we have decades of experience managing thousands of people, controlling millions of dollars, acquiring, merging, building, and selling companies. We built and dismantled organizations; managed start-ups and turnarounds; ran radio stations; produced television programs; created marketing and human resources departments; launched a national magazine; directed global human resources; assessed and coached senior executives; led, transitioned, and integrated acquisitions; designed and executed organizational restructurings and downsizings; served on corporate boards; and battled the competition. We have succeeded, failed, and succeeded again.

Nancy Widmann was inducted into the Broadcasting Hall of Fame in 2005 after a 25-year career at CBS. As president of CBS Radio for eight years, she led a team of talented executives and built her division into the most successful radio company in the industry. With responsibility for 1,200 people and over $400 million in sales, Nancy became expert at understanding how each division contributes to the financial lifeline of a corporation. Managing 21 radio stations and 6 radio networks within the CBS empire, Nancy learned first-hand that whatever your level in your organization, you're always in effect running for office, and that your survival depends not only on delivering the bottom line but on mastering the art of corporate politics.

Nancy's I-didn't-see-it-coming moment came just after Westinghouse bought CBS. She had known the company was on the block, but assumed that her long, successful run in the corner office would give her immunity and keep her at the helm of the division. After all, she had doubled the profits of CBS Radio, had a strong reputation in the industry, and was the only woman running a major division at CBS. But Westinghouse didn't see it that way. So when she heard the words, "They don't want you," from Peter Lund, former president of the CBS network, she was stunned. Westinghouse replaced Nancy with a senior executive on their own team, the president of Westinghouse Radio.

By contrast, much of Elaine Eisenman's career has been spent as a corporate outsider. She holds a doctorate in industrial and organizational psychology, and has spent over 25 years consulting for Fortune 500 companies, advising CEOs and their executive teams about organizational effectiveness and cultural change. Elaine holds and has held seats on several public and private boards. On many occasions, she temporarily assumed key executive roles for clients undergoing significant growth or cultural transformation. In those roles, both inside and out, she has been responsible for decisions that led others to say, "I didn't see it coming." Still, despite all that experience, Elaine had an I-didn't-see-it-coming event of her own.

While consulting for American Express, Elaine was asked to serve as a senior vice president of human resources, and to assist her visionary leader, the executive vice president, in redesigning the department. Two and a half years into the reorganization, Elaine got an unexpected call one evening from the chairman of the company, informing her that her boss had died. She was charged with managing the search for a new executive VP, but realized that the new boss might not have the same mandate as the former one. Elaine took on the assignment and completed it successfully, but left the company when the search was complete.

Amy Dorn Kopelan moved upward through the executive ranks of ABC Television for 20 years, and as senior vice president of morning television, she managed programming at *Good Morning America* for 9 years. Because of her ability to successfully manage teams of creative people, she was named executive vice president of direct marketing for ABC Entertainment, where she helped develop and launch *Episodes*, a national magazine.

Amy's I-didn't-see-it-coming moment came when ABC decided to shut down *Episodes*. Because of her incredible track record inside the company, Amy couldn't imagine that she wouldn't be offered another senior position. But that didn't happen. Instead, Dan Burke, COO of Capital Cities/ABC, candidly told Amy that, with her entrepreneurial talents, there was no suitable role for her in the company and that it was time for her to launch out on her own.

The three of us, each in her own way, emerged more knowledgeable, intuitive, savvy, and tough. Looking back, we realize that there were clear warning signs that our jobs were in jeopardy. Nancy misjudged the impact on her career of a pending sale; Elaine assumed that her solid contributions would outweigh her alliance to a former boss; and Amy didn't realize that with a new regime came a new set of mandates. We either hadn't seen the signs at all or completely ignored them. In the years since getting blindsided, each of us has had the opportunity to work with dozens of executives, almost all of whom had I-didn't-see-it-coming moments at one time or another.

What we've learned is that in business, survival is rarely about performance; almost everyone at the top levels of the organization is talented. Instead, it's about learning how to spot dangers before they arise and how to wage a campaign based on political savvy and smart strategy.

HOW THIS BOOK IS DIFFERENT

This book is intended for all executives, professionals, and managers—male or female—who are career-established and want to control and direct their success, to climb and survive in the new corporate America. While many other books target the same audience, our experiences in the trenches give us the perspective to talk about corporate survival from a vantage point that's usually overlooked. Other books lay out a recipe for success either based on the author's specific journey to the top or viewed through the lens of a theoretical business environment. But *I Didn't See It Coming* is a very different kind of book.

For one thing, we know first-hand how difficult it is to be confronted with the unexpected or to be caught off guard. And we are acutely aware of what it feels like to lose, even for a brief time, power or composure.

Second, *I Didn't See It Coming* is squarely focused on how to avoid being blindsided by changes of any kind within your organization. To achieve that goal we've taken our experience and hard-earned perspectives, coupled them with those of clients, colleagues, friends, and others whom we interviewed, and placed these observations and learnings into an organizational context. No other career book provides this kind of critical and experiential lens.

But most importantly, these stories are far more than simple cautionary tales. Instead, they provide a framework for thinking and acting that we wish we had had during tough times in our own careers. When Elaine conducts assessment interviews with clients, as they review their past challenges, she always asks, "With the gift of hindsight, what would you have done differently?" *I Didn't See*

It Coming is our gift of hindsight to you. Over the course of the rest of this book, we:

- Show you how to determine where the true power lies within your organization.
- Teach you to spot the land mines that emerge during corporate culture change.
- Give you the most effective strategies to neutralize potential danger.
- Help you steer a safe and profitable course over the risky corporate terrain of shifting alliances, backstabbing peers, and newcomer CEOs.
- Tell you what to watch out for, when to duck, when to bail, with whom to align, and even when and how to side step or even topple the boss.
- Help you develop the critical insights, effective tools, and instincts necessary to read any room, control your own career destiny, and outsmart the competition at every turn of the road.

MANAGING MINEFIELDS

Throughout this book we use the metaphor of a minefield to describe your organization. Sound harsh? We don't think so. We have observed, first-hand, how difficult it can be to maneuver without setting off hidden political land mines. Having a clear and safe path is critical to a sustainable career.

Here's a fascinating story: A Danish company, Areasa Biodetection, has been using genetic engineering to develop a land mine-detecting flower. This normally green plant will bloom red when its roots make contact with nitrogen dioxide, which degrading hidden land mines leak into the soil.[1] These small flowers are *nature's red flags*, identifying imminent danger. Until some smart bioengineers develop a *corporate* land mine-detecting flower, this book will play that role, helping you see the red flags, avoid the hidden dangers, and find safe passage.

The key to staying clear of the land mines is to master your relationships with the four types of critical players in organizational life: your employees, your peers, your boss, and senior staff. In our view, no matter where you sit in the organization, these four groups of people have the ultimate influence on your survival and success.

Before discussing the players, we start the book with something that may seem counterintuitive: creating an exit strategy, a strategic plan that lays out what you're going to do, where you're going to go, and how you're going to get there if your job starts going south. Think of it as a corporate prenup agreement. An exit strategy prepares you to make your next move or to walk out the door. With a well-developed exit strategy, you can lead, innovate, and challenge the status quo. A strong strategy positions you to deal boldly and securely with bosses, peers, employees, and senior staff. Putting yourself in charge of the endgame, you'll be able to make smarter decisions about managing your career and gain the confidence you need to move up the ladder.

Here are the some of the insights and counsel we bring you in the ensuing chapters:

- In Chapters 2 and 3, we talk about taking the reins, developing your leadership style, maintaining perspective, and evaluating your subordinates. We also share with you a number of critical observations relating to assessing talent, hiring, balancing relationships, and matching cultures.

- We devote Chapter 4 to a discussion of "you scratch my back, I'll scratch yours" politics, putting together a band of brothers or sisters who can give you insights, warnings, and feedback that will help you advance your career.

- In Chapter 5, we explain the dangers inherent in working on teams. But since it's almost impossible to avoid being on a team, we give you the tools you need to gain visibility, get credit, and psyche out the team dynamic.

- Chapter 6 is devoted to new bosses. We show you how to recognize when your current boss is on his way out as well as strategies to navigate through the chaos that reigns after the old boss has packed his bags and the new one starts unpacking.

- Everyone, regardless of their place on the food chain, has a boss. In Chapter 7, we share with you how to manage yours by making her look good, and how to be ever so careful not to outshine her. We also discuss the need to protect her back, and the dangers of being too closely allied with a boss.

- In Chapter 8, we change our focus to the world of senior staff, the folks who have no profit-and-loss responsibilities but who wield a tremendous amount of power. We show you how these hidden influents, with a direct line to the CEO, can support or impede your climb to the top. As an added bonus, we help you deal with consultants so that you can leverage them to your own benefit.

- Chapter 9 is a candid and eye-opening discussion of how to identify sea change inside your organization and how to recognize when your career may be coming to a crashing halt. We provide a no-fault game plan for effectively handling the day of reckoning and maintaining power and composure through the process. Lastly, we articulate our four laws for preventing an I-didn't-see-it-coming moment.

CAN YOU SEE IT COMING?

When you look at the big picture, it's not hard to understand why so many wise and experienced executives never see it coming—and why so many don't have an exit strategy. Reading signals and connecting dots on the business landscape can be confusing. What's more, no one really wants to consider that his or her career or position could be in jeopardy. So we often block out, ignore, or misinterpret what we'd rather not see at all. Or we observe the signs, but subconsciously we don't let them register.

As we see it, the problem here has to do with two significant needs: personal identity and social predictability. Despite warnings from psychologists and career coaches, most executives tie their identity to their job. *They are what they do.* The lines blur; they become the job. At cocktail parties, no one says "I work at being a marketing executive." They say, "I *am* a marketing executive." When that identity is threatened—when the "who I am" might be at risk—it's easy to ignore the warning signals, particularly when they hint that you might lose position or power. Self-protection becomes the order of the day, instead of a savvy assessment of what is happening around you.

We all crave predictability. We need to know where we're going on Monday morning. If we're heading into the office, we have a pretty good idea of what our colleagues will want to discuss, what our assistants will ask us, and what the boss will be looking for. We all rely on consistent patterns and find it hard to give them up. Even the most powerful executive craves and depends on a certain predictability and normalcy that gives structure to his life and creates a familiar social network.

When that predictability and social network are threatened, being objective and insightful in the face of danger becomes difficult, if not impossible. That's exactly when we're most likely to get blindsided. Since people have intense needs and a great deal invested in their personal success, job satisfaction, and career goals, they can't possibly accept that this could all come to a precipitous end.

Our goal in this book is not to place you in a constant state of anxiety and paranoia, but rather to give you the tools you need to step up, charge forward, and reach the top without getting blindsided. Learning to see those red flags will guide and inform every decision you make. It will also give you the power to be a confident and creative leader.

Let's get started!

1

EXIT STRATEGIES AND WHY YOU NEED ONE

Betty Taylor pushed the elevator button. She was on her way to meet with her boss, Peter Grometti, chairman of the company, and she had a good idea what they were going to be talking about. Grometti was chairman of Marcus Publishing and had just closed the deal to sell the company to LDGT, a large holding company that owned magazines, newspapers, and broadcast properties. Betty was president of consumer magazines, a position she had held for 10 years, during which time she had doubled the readership and profits.

Betty walked into the meeting fully expecting to take over the acquiring company's magazine division, and was excited about the prospect of increasing her responsibilities and power in the industry, but the conversation with Grometti took her completely by surprise. In a quiet and firm voice, he told her that the new owners didn't want her to stay on. Instead, they expected her to shut down operations, dismiss most of her staff, and leave the company in six months. It was really very simple: They already had a president of consumer magazines, he was their guy, and they wanted him to run the combined operation.

As Grometti continued on with the details, Betty realized that her whole life was about to change. As she rode the elevator back down to her floor, she began to take stock. She hadn't looked at her contract in years, hadn't taken a call from a headhunter in over eight months. Even worse, she had stopped actively networking as her travel and workload had taken over and consumed her life. She realized that she just *hadn't seen it coming* and, even worse, had no idea what to do.

Are you prepared to react quickly to major changes within your organization? If you were to lose your job tomorrow, how prepared would you be? Are you ready to walk if the writing on the wall is unacceptable? We posed these questions to CEOs, presidents, and senior executives of Fortune 500 companies at several large symposia in the United States and Canada. Amazingly, none of those leaders—not a single one—had a plan in place. And it gets worse: None of them had spent any time thinking about where they would go next, what kind of work they'd find fulfilling, or even whether they were prepared emotionally or financially to leave their company.

To sum up, none of these executives, no matter what their level, had what we call an *exit strategy*—a well-thought-out, tactical plan that prepares you for making your next move and gives you control over your career no matter what happens. You wouldn't allow your division, department, or company to simply run along aimlessly, without a forward-focused business plan that includes several contingency scenarios, would you? The same should be true of your job. If you don't have an exit strategy, you're effectively abandoning control of your career and leaving your future flapping in the wind. Without an exit strategy you're jeopardizing your—and your family's—fiscal and psychological health.

There are several key reasons why every executive, at every level of his or her career, needs an exit strategy. We often refer to them as the three Cs:

1. *Change.* No matter how long you've been with your current employer or how secure you feel, no job is permanent. We have seen, time and time again, proof that the old adage, "Change is the only constant," is true. To compete in today's tumultuous marketplace, companies that have any dream of growing must continually innovate. And we're not talking about just coming up with new and better *products.* Innovation also includes streamlining processes and hiring the people who can help you meet the new challenges you'll face as you move forward. Unfortunately, with the new reality of mergers, acquisitions, downsizing, and restructuring, many managers, no matter how experienced or skilled they are, will find themselves left by the side of the road. Now, don't get us wrong; we're not trying to convince you that you're always one short step away from the unemployment line—not at all. We just want you to be aware that things can change overnight, and that those changes may require you to reinvent yourself.

2. *Confidence.* It is impossible to be a truly creative, innovative, out-of-the-box leader if you're afraid of losing your job. Knowing exactly what you'd do if the ax suddenly dropped gives you a sense of security that allows you to lead more effectively. A viable exit strategy gives you the confidence to say, "What's the worst that can happen? I'm ready to leave if this doesn't work." If you're not completely confident that you can survive for a while without this job, you won't have the courage to take the risks necessary for success.

3. *Control.* An exit strategy puts you in control of your professional life. It's a take-charge policy. It gives you the opportunity to be on a path that you choose, not one that others have chosen for you. Being in control affords you the chance and security to make career decisions in your own best interest.

So, it's all about handling risks. Growth occurs from calculated risk, and you can't truly move forward in your career without taking a chance. Yet, at the same time, if you are afraid that you could lose your job and be out on the street, you cannot take risks. In today's turbulent marketplace it's critical to have a smart, savvy plan for moving ahead—whether it's to a new position in your company or out the door entirely. Once that plan is in place, it will shape the way you respond to bosses, peers, subordinates, shareholders, boards of directors, and everyone else. And, most important, it will allow you to do what you think is necessary in the service of growth—both yours and your company's.

AN EXIT STRATEGY: WHAT IT IS AND ISN'T

Let's get this out of the way right now. A severance package is *not* an exit strategy. A severance package, which covers the terms of disengagement, may be the *culmination* of an effective exit strategy, but that will be determined only *after* the rest of your strategy is firmly in place. In addition, an exit strategy is *not* just a plan to leave your current company, and it doesn't have to be a terminal farewell.

So, what is it? An exit strategy is simply a long-term plan that sets a course for your career. It answers the question "What's next?" What all executives must realize is that you shouldn't be asking that question only after you get downsized or something else happens *to* you. It is often best to ask what's next when your career is moving forward successfully.

Let's say, for example, that you were part of a team that just finished rescuing a failing division and, in the process, you realized that you have a passion for turnaround work. It provides the kind of challenge you love and, best of all, you're incredibly good at it. But what happens when the turnaround is over and you find yourself back in your old job—a job you used to love but that now doesn't give you that rush? When you find yourself in a situation where your goals and skills are no longer in alignment with your job description, having a well-crafted exit strategy gives you the tools and safety net you need to move—inside or outside your company.

Thus, an exit strategy is a framework for thinking about next steps. In addition, it helps you articulate a vision of your future and what you hope to achieve throughout your career. To maximize your choices and options, this framework sets the basis for thinking about what those goals look like and what they require.

CREATING YOUR EXIT STRATEGY

Putting together an exit strategy—or any other strategic plan—isn't something that you do once and walk away from. It's a plan that's constantly evolving, one that requires continual revision and refining.

It also requires an ongoing level of awareness and insight into the environment in which you operate, which means you'll need to stay completely up-to-date on changes, major and minor, within your organization, including shifts in management structure, reorganizations, consolidations, layoffs, share price, earnings reports, and so on. You'll need to be aware of any and all external forces that could affect your company, such as mergers, acquisitions, economic forecasts, interest rate changes, what your competitors are doing, and how your industry sector is performing overall. You should be on top of all these things anyway. This kind of knowledge is critical to being an informed and aware executive. We are suggesting that you crank it up a notch.

If this sounds like a lot of work, you're right; it is. However, a well-put-together exit strategy is such a critical survival tool that we encourage you to make it a top priority. It does *not*, of course, have to be the centerpiece of your life, and you don't need to spend hours on it every day, but it should be in the back of your mind. Always consider how day-to-day events might affect your company. As you read the *Wall Street Journal* or trade publications that focus on your business, ask yourself whether what you're reading could possibly affect you and your job, and how. Do the same thing when you go to trade shows or meet with colleagues from other companies. Pick up tidbits of information, put them together, and figure out that something is happening or about to happen. All of this gathering and updating of information serves as the basic foundation for your exit strategy.

As the old saying goes, "If you don't know where you're going, you won't know when you get there." You should always have some idea where you want to go next and what it will take to get you there. Remember, the plan is fluid. Decisions you make about your exit strategy or your next step may change in response to internal or external events. You can't let your exit strategy become stagnant or rigid, and you shouldn't lock yourself into a single path. Have short-term goals, think regularly about long-term goals, and then remember that life happens.

Every strong, effective exit strategy must include the following four elements:

1. Create an exit fund.
2. Organize a personal board of directors.
3. Increase your professional marketability.
4. Leverage your networks.

Create an Exit Fund

One of the most important, and most ignored, pieces of advice financial planners give their client is to set aside a financial reserve that can cover all their expenses for a given period of time—usually 6 to 12 months. We agree, but suggest you think in terms of a minimum of 12 to 18 months. Why the extra padding? Because if your exit strategy turns into a severance package, there's a good chance that you'll have to do more than just pay your mortgage and put food on the table. This is especially true if you're intending to do something entrepreneurial. Having a good chunk of cash or liquid assets allows you the freedom to gamble on a new career or to try a new business path where there may be less financial stability. Resist the temptation to dip into your fund for any reason other than getting you through a period of unemployment or underemployment. There could be circumstances beyond your control that keep you on the bench longer than you anticipated.

We made creating an exit fund item number one because, without it, you'll never have the freedom to respond to change in a decisive way. If you ever detect trouble brewing within your organization and want to make a career change, or find the decision made for you, knowing you have the financial security to last a while can make all the difference in the world.

Everyone's situation is different and, unfortunately, there's no magic formula for building a contingency fund like the one we're suggesting; but even if there were, this isn't a book about financial planning. So, let's leave it at this: Sock away as much as you possibly can. If you need help structuring a plan, don't hesitate to ask your accountant or financial advisor.

Organize a Personal Board of Directors

Whether you're a CEO, entrepreneur, or manager in a large organization, you didn't get there all by yourself, and you're not going to make your next career move by yourself, either. That's why we encourage you to organize a *personal board of directors*, a group of trusted advisers who will be your go-to people whenever you need advice or direction about your career. These can include your attorney, accountant, mentor, career counselor, or a friend in the executive search business.

The idea here is to include people who know you, your strengths, your weaknesses, and your potential but who are not emotionally or financially tied to the outcome of your decisions. You need objective, yet concerned, members for this board. Does that mean that your spouse isn't right for the job? It depends. Too many spouses—although they'll never admit it—have an agenda, and may secretly (or not so secretly) value financial security more than your personal or professional satisfaction. What about a parent or a sibling? Again, it depends. If they've got the right professional affiliations, they can sometimes be enormously helpful, but you need to be able to trust their objectivity. What's most important is that your personal board be made up of people from *outside* your company. We'll talk about banding together with people *inside* your company in Chapter 4.

The trait you want all of your personal directors to have is a proven ability to help you think things through. You also want directors who can provide guidance if you sense corporate upheaval, or who can brainstorm about possible changes in your career path. Ideally, they would all be reachable when you need them but, since they've got jobs and other obligations, you should be flexible on that requirement. Keeping your go-to list current, and talking to your advisers on a regular basis, is an important part of a viable exit strategy.

We often talk with our clients about creating a personal board of directors. Here are four questions that frequently come up.

1. *How do I ask someone to serve on my board?* Most people are flattered to be asked. When you tell people that you respect their judgment and value their opinion, there's a very good chance that they'll agree to guide you when you have an opportunity to explore or a situation to resolve. So, in most cases, this doesn't have to be much more complicated than calling people you can trust and asking them to be available to offer advice when you need their professional perspective.

2. *How formal or informal should my board be?* In our experience, most personal boards of directors are pretty informal. But this is *your* board and *your* future, so make it any way you'd like, just be sure to staff it with people you can trust and who you know will give you good advice if you need it. Keep in mind that unlike corporate boards, there aren't any contracts to sign, and you probably won't have meetings that all your directors will attend. Instead, depending on where your board members live and how immediate your situation, you'll either meet with them by phone or individually.

3. *How often should I change the members of the board?* Your board's composition and the qualifications of its members will change over time and in response to your personal and professional growth. Attrition will happen naturally as you find that you have less need for some kinds of skills and more for others. Most people have a mix of permanent and

temporary or rotating members. And you can, of course, add to your board when you feel the need for more expertise in a particular arena.

4. *Should I compensate people on my board?* A personal board of directors doesn't expect direct compensation. It would be nice to invite members to dinner, buy them gifts for a special celebration, make a donation to a favorite charity, or offer to serve on *their* personal boards.

Increase Your Marketability

Take a minute now and think about where you want your career to be in the next two years. Be sure to consider salary and other compensation, job title and responsibilities, and stature. Assuming that your goals are realistic, ask yourself this question: Do I have the qualifications, education, training, and experience to make those goals a reality?

Chances are, your honest answer is *no*. If it weren't, you'd have already accomplished your goals. Given that fact, what is it going to take to get you where you want to be? Once you have that figured out, you should ask yourself the two most important questions of all:

1. Will acquiring all those skills and education make me as marketable as I must be to make the next move?
2. What other training or experience do I need in order to position myself to react quickly and land on my feet if I come back from lunch tomorrow and my boss gives me 15 minutes to clear out my desk?

What you do to increase your marketability can run the gamut from taking courses in a foreign language to pursuing your MBA. It shouldn't stop there. Consider yourself a work in progress and never stop trying to improve and upgrade what, whom, and how much you know. The more you improve your professional resume, the better prepared you'll be to act quickly in the face of a merger, a new boss arriving on the scene, or downsizing that can threaten your current position.

Anna Houser is a perfect example of someone who honed her skills in anticipation of change. Anna was the corporate senior vice president of communications at a major movie studio but had always dreamed of being on the creative side of the business. Since her staff job didn't provide the creative challenge she was looking for, Anna assumed that if she were ever going to be able to pursue her goals she would eventually have to leave her company. So she enrolled in film production courses at UCLA and volunteered to work nights on the back lot of her company's studio. Within 10 months Anna had earned an associate's degree in film and had acquired a lot of hands-on production experience.

Then, out of the blue, her company was taken over by a large competitor, and Anna was smart enough to know that the acquiring company would come onto the scene with its own staff professionals and that she'd probably be out of a job. Armed with her degree and her production credentials, she asked to meet with the new head of production, and successfully landed a new job in the documentary film unit. Unlike most of her colleagues, Anna made the move from a staff job to the creative side of the business and was not blindsided by the sale of her company. Most of her colleagues weren't so lucky—or so smart.

Leverage Your Networks

Developing networks takes time and focus. Keeping in touch is hard work, but it's a critical component of your exit strategy. We all have a *network*—the key is learning to leverage it. What is a network? It's the web of connections that link us to other people. No matter where you work or what role you have inside your company, you have a network you can begin to tap into. Actually, you probably have two: a formal one and an informal one.

Your formal network consists of organized groups of people, such as members of your church or synagogue, trade groups, alumni associations, and Rotary. Being involved in organizations like these gives you some visibility, and the connections you make at their meetings or public events will give you access to a lot of information on a regular basis. The more involved you get, the more information—and the more opportunities—you'll have. Serving as an officer or board member puts you in position to show off more of your talents. When people are impressed by your efforts, enthusiasm, and presentation, they'll be more inclined to let you know if they hear of appropriate opportunities and to recommend you for new positions. The unique value of the formal network is that people *outside* of your company will get to see you in action and they'll know that you can really make things happen.

Your informal network is more loosely made up of the people you work with; the friends, associates, and colleagues you have lunch with; and anyone else who might have a contact that could be valuable to you. Outside of your company, your informal network is a great source of business tips, introductions, referrals, and favors. Inside the company, it's that famous grapevine that people seem to hear so much through. Think of it as an early warning system that can let you know about promotions, job openings, dismissals, and power shifts.

If you don't leverage your informal network, you won't be able to expand your nexus. Elaine Eisenman often says that whenever she is ready to move on in her career, she throws out to the universe her desire to move, and the universe answers. This is not as easy or glib as it seems. It is hard work because she begins the process by envisioning her next step and then identifies all the people she knows who might be able to put her in touch with people who know the people to get her to that next step. This is what it takes to leverage your network.

Margie Sternberg, a relatively new VP of human resources at a major telecom company, is a great example of someone who reaped the benefits of having created strong formal and informal networks. Margie reported to the executive VP of human resources, who made no secret of the fact that she intended to stay in her position until her retirement 10 years down the line. But Margie wanted to take on more responsibility and learn more about her field, and she wisely decided it would be a mistake to tread water until her boss retired.

Margie had always had a strong sense of community service and had volunteered at a number of local charities for years. As a result, she had developed a large informal network of people outside of her company that she could ask about new opportunities where she could apply her talents and interests. Her network tipped her off about an opening at a large New York not-for-profit agency, and she was able to use those contacts to line up an interview with the head of the agency. Although she had no formal training in fund-raising, Margie's HR experience, volunteer activity, and technical skills made her a perfect candidate. Several weeks later, she landed the job.

Search firms are also a type of network, and even if you aren't looking for work, whenever a headhunter calls, your first response should always be, "Hold on while I close the door." Talking to headhunters on a regular basis can help you develop relationships that you'll be able to leverage if you ever need to. It's also a great way to do some informal market research. Because they talk to so many people, headhunters pick up all sorts of juicy bits of information and they're often aware of changes or developing trends in your industry long before they become public. But you won't have access to that information if you don't take the calls or you don't share information of your own. If someone you know is looking for a job, or if some executive in your company just got fired, let the headhunter know (unless, of course, the information is proprietary). Developing and maintaining these connections is another vital part of your exit strategy, because some day, when you really need the help, they may refer you for your next job.

There are several other ways to build your networks. Here are two of our favorites—and they really work:

1. Whenever people give you business cards or an e-mail address or ask you for something, contact them within 24 hours and either respond to their request or try to give them some information they're looking for. This could be as simple as where to purchase something, a restaurant address, or a phone number of a colleague.
2. Once a week, make it a point to meet with someone socially, be it for breakfast, lunch, or dinner, to ask

them how they got their job. It's easier to invite someone you know rather than someone you just met, although one of the best ways to move people from the category of "just met" to "know well" is to take them out for coffee or a meal. Each time you meet with someone, ask them to suggest three other people you can either meet with or call to learn more about a different industry or company with which you're unfamiliar. Then stand back and watch how quickly your network grows!

NEGOTIATING THE END AT THE BEGINNING

Just as having an exit strategy gives you the courage to take risks and lead more effectively, having control over what happens when everything falls apart provides an extra psychological and financial safeguard. What we're talking about here is the severance package: the financial plan that kicks in when you leave your employer. For example, if you're jumping into a new venture or coming in to be part of a major restructuring, you may be able to pre-arrange an increased payout if things go awry.

This is what we call a *corporate prenup*, and it's the ultimate survival weapon. It's actually not too different from a marital prenup, and the message on the table is basically the same: "We all want this to work; we plan on a productive and successful relationship and a great partnership. But just in case things don't go as we planned, we want to be very clear on the terms of the 'divorce.'"

Unfortunately, too many managers and executives are afraid to go this route. They worry that suggesting a sever-

16

ance agreement *up front* indicates that (1) they don't trust the new organization, (2) they don't have confidence in their new boss, or (3) they don't believe that they'll be successful in their new role.

Nothing could be further from the truth. Spelling out the terms in advance gives everyone involved full disclosure and helps employer and employee to better understand each other's expectations. Working out a severance package up front is one of the wisest and most respected negotiating tactics you can employ, and it has a number of benefits. The most obvious one, of course, is that it makes your exit strategy almost bulletproof.

As smart as it is to negotiate the end at the beginning, it's even smarter to let an objective party negotiate for you. Since you probably don't have an agent, you should consider an attorney or financial adviser. The main thing is to have someone from outside the company who will look out for your best interest. It's neither a hostile nor a defensive role. If your new boss or the HR people balk at the idea, tell them that because these discussions frequently become contentious, you feel that having someone else there can help deflect the emotions.

If, for whatever reason, you're not able to negotiate a prenup before starting a job, you absolutely must get a copy of the corporate severance policy. As with the prenup itself, asking for the policy doesn't indicate any lack of trust or enthusiasm on your part. You're simply doing intelligent due diligence, which should show your new boss that you're confident, secure, and not afraid to ask tough questions.

Sam Eiler successfully negotiated a corporate prenup before signing on to a large corporation, and it saved his career. Sam had been a management consultant for years when one of his clients, a major consumer products firm, offered him a job as a senior VP. Sam was excited about the opportunity to work for a chairman who for years had been impressed with his consulting work. Because he had done strategic planning for the company, Sam knew more about the position and its responsibilities than most new executives would. He saw the newly created position as a challenging and potentially lucrative opportunity, but before closing his consulting practice to take the job, he asked his attorney to negotiate a detailed prenup. His rationale was that by shutting down his business he was taking a significant risk. And by asking the company to shoulder some risk of their own, everyone would have a greater desire and incentive to make the new arrangement work.

Three months into the job, Sam realized he had made a terrible mistake. His newly hired team was running into constant roadblocks and progress was happening at a glacial pace. He realized that the culture of the company, entrenched in tradition, would simply not allow him to move the business in the direction that the chairman had promised. To make matters worse, support from the corner office was lukewarm at best. This was clearly not the job he had signed on for. Sam decided to give it another couple of months, but by the time he hit the half-year mark the situation had only gotten worse. With his prenup locked in place, Sam had the conviction to submit his resignation to the chairman and exercise his severance package.

The lesson here is clear and simple. No matter how firm the handshake when you assume the new title and role, negotiating up front should be *standard operating procedure*. When you've negotiated the end at the beginning, you won't ever have to put up with a situation that puts you and your future at risk.

CHAPTER 1   Takeaways

1. Create an exit strategy to help you manage *change*, increase your *confidence*, and put you in *control* of your professional life.

2. Don't confuse an exit strategy with a severance package. They are not the same. The exit strategy is a "next step" formal plan.

3. Continually revise, refine, and update your exit strategy; it isn't a one-shot deal.

4. Set aside a financial reserve to see you through at least a year of unemployment. This is called an *exit fund*.

5. Organize a personal board of directors who will serve as your go-to people.

6. Work to increase your professional marketability.

7. Leverage your formal and informal networks.

8. Negotiate a corporate prenup before you start a new job.

2

TAKING THE REINS

Congratulations! Your skills and competence have finally been recognized and now *you're* running the show. Having stood exactly where you are, we know how tempting it is to go out and celebrate. But don't do it yet. If you simply can't resist, at least keep the festivities low-key and away from the office. Whether you've had your key to the executive washroom for a while, or this is your first venture into a senior executive role, you're probably feeling a mixture of exhilaration and apprehension. That's perfectly normal, and if you're planning to keep moving up through the ranks, you'd better get used to it. Because as you get closer to that top-floor, corner office, the stakes keep getting higher, the competition tougher and more intense, and the mistakes more costly. In our experience, if you get too caught up with your new success, you won't be able to prepare yourself to lead, really understand your new responsibilities, and keep yourself from being blindsided. And you have a limited amount of time to do that. So accept your congratulations with humility and grace and read on.

A SMART START

Most newly promoted managers believe that they need to jump into their new position with a bang—so they call a staff meeting, start to evaluate the troops, and begin poring over the numbers. We can't think of a better way to start off on the wrong foot. Instead, we suggest that you move a couple of other items to the top of your priority list:

1. Stop and think about why senior management chose *you* for your new job.
2. Recognize that your real source of power comes from the people who report to you.

Let's take a look what makes these two points so critical and why ignoring them can trip you up. Pay close attention—otherwise that bang you're hoping to hear could be the sound of your chances for future promotions blowing up.

Why Me?

You didn't wind up in your new position because of your charm and good looks, although neither one hurts. Senior management picked you for the job because they think you have the skill set necessary to do the job they want done. It's up to you to find out in a hurry what, exactly, that job is and what you're expected to deliver. If you don't, you can't possibly succeed, and that greatly increases your chances of being blindsided later. Here are some examples of the kinds of questions you should be asking yourself:

- Have they asked me to take over because I can fix the operation?
- Have they put me in this job to maintain the status quo?
- Am I here to revamp, shake it up, or start over?
- Are they looking for a negotiator? A diplomat? A hatchet man?
- How is upper management defining success? Are there certain targets I'm expected to meet? How quickly do they want to see results?

It is essential that you determine why you were put in the job and what your marching orders are as soon as possible. To be successful, you need a plan for your first 90 days, and no achievable plan is possible unless you have answers to these questions. Armed with goals and objectives, you'll be able to run the show more effectively and give your new bosses confidence that they made the right choice in naming you to the position.

Power Defies Gravity

Unlike what you may have learned in high school about water, power flows *uphill*. Why should this matter to you? Because no one leads in a vacuum, and if the people who work for you don't buy into your vision, and don't trust you as a leader, you'll never get the support you need to accomplish your mission. This is a vitally important point;

if you can't get the troops to charge up the hill behind you, you will eventually fail.

Okay. Now that you know why you got the job and how you're going to be evaluated, and you understand that you can't do the job alone, it's time to schedule that first big staff meeting.

SETTING THE COURSE

From the time the previous boss announced he was leaving until the day you formally take the reins, people in your new area or new company have been anxious about who you are and what the "messiah" will bring. Even if you were promoted from within, your new staff may not know what goals or standards you might set. Until these questions are answered for them and their anxiety is reduced, work will suffer. In the absence of real information, people tend to create their own explanations. And the longer the uncertainty continues, the more widespread and firmly fixed those made-up facts become. The only way to stop the confusion and noise is to tell people right up front exactly what your plans are and what you expect from them. If you wait too long, you'll find yourself spending valuable time quashing rumors instead of focusing on your vision and strategy. The way you articulate goals defines your leadership style and telegraphs what it will be like to work for you.

Here are a few examples of approaches that new managers have taken to address their assembled staffs.

- *Hold a town hall meeting.* Nancy Widmann worked for an executive at CBS who addressed her team by first acknowledging that she knew they had many questions for their new boss. She also was aware that people might be reluctant to stand up and ask tough questions in front of colleagues. She prepared a Q&A session where she presented both the questions *and the answers* on a wide range of topics that she anticipated her new staff wanted to discuss. This process created an atmosphere of candor, and reduced a lot of tension. It also gave everyone in the room permission to dive in and ask even more questions that might have otherwise been kept under wraps.

- *Encourage innovation.* Amy Kopelan met Alice, an executive at a New York not-for-profit institute who told her new staff that every project they launched or designed should be considered a pilot program. As long as the results of these initiatives were well considered, if the initiative failed, it would be seen as a learning experience and no one would be criticized for the lack of success. Her goal was to create a climate where everyone on her staff felt invested in the division's success, was willing to think of and suggest alternatives to the status quo, and was excited to come to work. And she succeeded. Sure, there were a few flops along the way, but they were more than offset by the home runs. Best of all, Alice was able to create an environment that was ripe with innovation.

- *Support risk-taking.* Elaine Eisenman, in her role as a consultant, sat in on a meeting with a media company COO who told his new senior managers that he wanted all of them to take a significant new-business risk during their first month on the job. If the attempt failed, it would be applauded, not criticized. This manager recognized that he needed his new staff scouring the marketplace for new opportunities in order to grow the company. He had to put a safety net under his people so they would feel free to jump on the high wire and take risks without fear of falling.

Clearing the Air

All three of the setting-the-record-straight approaches just described were somewhat nontraditional but still produced outstanding results. In addition, they had one very important thing in common: They all created a climate where employees could thrive and take calculated risks, a climate of candor, credibility, and clarity—especially clarity. If you're looking for a way to get the most out of your team, ensure their support, and solidify your power, you'll do the same. The alternative—an environment based on fear, or where messages are muddled or unclear—is guaranteed to fail, because indecisive or secretive leaders are never able to coalesce the troops.

There's one important thing to remember about clarity. You may be 120 percent clear on your goals and expectations, and 150 percent clear when it comes to expressing those goals and expectations and getting your team solidly behind you. But if the various layers of management above you aren't clear—either in their own minds or everyone else's—you're in big trouble. In cases like this (and they aren't as rare as you might think), ensuring clarity becomes *your* responsibility. In other words, you may have to step in and manage the rank above you.

Here's an example where there was no organizational clarity offered by senior management, no clarity of role for team leaders, and no clarity of responsibility—all in all, a surefire way to undermine effective leadership. Jane

Mannes, former VP of human resources, was promoted to senior VP of human resources at a large glass manufacturing company. Human resources had always been part of the legal department, which was headed by Dan Morales, general counsel and senior VP. At the strong suggestion of the board of directors, the CEO spun human resources out of the legal department into its own stand-alone division, reporting directly to him. The CEO chose Jane, who had been a top employment lawyer in the company, to head this new division. The CEO dragged his feet on making a formal announcement, however, because he knew Dan would resist the reorganization.

Even though Jane had no prior management experience, she had enough savvy to see a minefield ahead. She understood that it was critical for her and her staff to have clarity about her new expanded role inside the company. She knew she had to establish a clear message of authority in order to lead her troops. And Jane knew it had to come from the CEO's office. Without the CEO's public support and a defined mandate, she couldn't take command, or communicate top management's objectives to her team. Internal chaos and confusion would reign.

The CEO was not a strong leader and feared confrontation. So Jane, on her own, prepared a formal announcement of the corporate realignment and asked the CEO to approve it. Before the announcement was issued or made public, Jane met with Dan. She had two main objectives. First, she wanted to get his support and advice on expediting the separation of the two departments. Second, she wanted to make sure that Dan himself wouldn't be blindsided by the public announcement. Jane effectively leveraged a complex situation in order to establish a clear vision of her role and create a mandate for her department.

The essence of organizational savvy is first to establish yourself and your role. Unlike Jane, you'll most likely have a boss who will guide you into your new role and help you get your footing as you grab the reins. But if you don't, it's up to you to take control!

Define Your Style

Recognizing that you have a distinct management style, and knowing how it affects others, is a critical component for shoring up your position and your success in a new role. If you've hit a senior leadership level in your company, you probably have a good fix on your style, but you may not be aware of its impact on your subordinates. It makes sense to identify or better confirm your own style by talking to former bosses, colleagues, and past direct reports. Also consider the opinion of a spouse and/or significant other. They often have valuable insights that are not apparent to anyone else. How would these people describe you?

- What are your strengths as a leader?

- What are your blind spots?

- What type of people work effectively with/for you?

- What kind of boss do you best respond to?

- Do you advocate structure or do you encourage a casual work environment?

- Do you need to be a star or do you reward others for their contribution?

If you want to succeed when you take on a new role, not only do you have to be cognizant of your management style, but you also have to recognize how your style of doing business impacts your new staff. Even though subordinates know that they'll have to adjust to a new boss's management style, if yours is markedly different from your predecessor's, we suggest that you introduce your style one step at a time. If not, there could be resistance. Take the case of our friend, Charlie Spencer.

Charlie was recruited to run a small graphic design company in Tulsa, Oklahoma. The company was made up of sales personnel, artists, and printers. Charlie replaced Harold McGuirk, who had been president for almost 20 years. Harold's style was formal, rigid, and distant. If any of the staff wanted to see Mr. McGuirk, they had to make an appointment. He rarely left his office and used an intercom system to communicate with his subordinates. Still, the company ran well, was profitable, and the staff seemed generally happy.

Charlie, on the other hand, was an open, accessible, friendly person. And he made the decision to use his style rather than imitate Harold's. Assuming everyone would welcome his manner, he asked people to call him Charlie and suggested that they "pop in" to see him any time they had questions, problems, or concerns. From day one, he roamed the halls, stopping at people's desks along the way, walking into offices. He had used this approach successfully at his former company and thought it would be a good way to hit the ground running in his new job, to see how things worked, and to get to know the staff.

But just a few days into Charlie's tenure, the company's productivity came to a screeching halt. The artists stopped drawing, presses slowed, and salespeople made fewer calls because they wanted to be in the office in case Charlie happened to stop by. And since no one had any idea what Charlie was looking for, people covered the papers and reports on their desk anytime he was in the neighborhood. Charlie was stupefied! Finally his assistant, Pat, summoned up the courage to pop into Charlie's office and announce to him that he was driving everyone crazy.

Although he had the best of intentions, Charlie tried to change the culture too quickly. McGuirk had been cold and distant, but at least the staff knew what to expect from him. Charlie learned that even though he came into his new job with a previously effective style for leading a team, it takes time to establish trust and credibility with subordinates. Moving too quickly can thwart the efforts of your staff and disrupt productivity, not enhance it.

Unfortunately, there's no single management style that will be successful in every organization. As we saw with McGuirk, just about any style can be effective, as long as the leader is authentic and consistent. Marie Mason, an executive we knew at NBC, described her style as a "benevolent dictatorship." She made it clear to her staff that she was not running a democracy, but that she'd attentively listen to everyone's ideas and concerns, and then make the decision she judged best. There was always active discussion, but never a group vote. Marie felt very strongly that you could not successfully run a division by consensus. Benevolent dictatorship worked in her case because this was a leader with strong vision in a highly competitive business who was willing to listen to ideas and suggestions but knew that the ultimate responsibility for results was hers. It was a style that fit the ethos of that organization. (*Ethos* is perhaps best defined as culture, a company's look, value system, and most importantly, its way of doing business. We will talk more extensively about that in Chapter 3.)

Daniel Goleman, in his work on emotional intelligence, found that the most effective executives have a repertoire of behavior-driving leadership skills that they use based on both the needs of the employees and the situation at hand.[1] This kind of "situational leadership" has also been advanced by industrial psychologist Dr. Paul Hersey, who has found that the most effective leaders are able to adapt their style to both the skill and readiness level of their followers.[2]

Mastering the Art of Not Knowing

As the new leader, you don't have to have all the answers. In fact, one of the most powerful and meaningful statements you can make is, "I don't know." No one is promoted because he knows the answers to every question. People are promoted because they're smart enough to know where to go to get those answers. You're no exception. So as you think about moving up the corporate or organizational ladder, remember that you're going to be promoted for your leadership, strategic thinking, and seasoned judgment, not for your specific technical or product knowledge.

When Nancy Widmann served as president of CBS Radio, she continually had to approve decisions about buying new equipment for the company's stations around the country: new antennae, control room boards, digital components, and the like. Because Nancy's background was in sales, no one expected her to be a technical expert. But her VP of engineering, Tony Massiello, *was* a technical expert, and he was the one Nancy relied on to help her make the right equipment buying decisions. Whenever a purchase request came in from one of the stations, Nancy would ask Tony two main questions: "Can you draw me a picture of what it does?" and "On a scale of 1 to 10, how critical is this equipment to the station's success?" Based on Tony's knowledge and expertise, Nancy was confident that she was making the right decisions.

This story demonstrates two important principles: (1) admit what you don't know, and (2) know whom to trust to find it out.

Are you worried that admitting you don't know could put you in jeopardy with your management? Don't be. To paraphrase Clint Eastwood in his role as Dirty Harry, "You've got to know your limitations." Honestly admitting that you don't know gives you enormous credibility; your staff will appreciate the fact that you know you don't have all the answers.

A former senior executive at one of the television networks used to warn that you should never sit in a meeting and nod your head as if you understand what is going on if you really don't. It doesn't make you smart; it makes you foolish. He suggested that if you let your insecurity or your arrogance get in the way, you'll never be seen as someone whom the team can trust to lead them with clarity and honesty. The key here is not to feign ignorance as a means of building loyalty, but rather to be authentic about your strengths and shortcomings. You set the stage for a climate of respect.

Asking questions is another important strategy, but if you don't *listen* to the answers, you set yourself up to be blindsided. We've all seen leaders who ostensibly listen just for the appearance of it. When a leader does that, it's nearly impossible to establish a climate of trust. It's immediately transparent. The smart move is to always listen attentively, evaluate the suggestions that are presented to you, ask follow-up questions to ensure you have the information you need to make the right decisions, and determine which solutions best accomplish your goals.

This was a lesson that Mark Levine didn't learn. Mark was a very competent guy who worked for a packaged goods company in Philadelphia. Over the course of 10 years, he steadily advanced through the ranks, finally becoming president of his division. And that's where his past caught up with him.

The problem was that Mark had developed a reputation as someone who only pretended to listen to his staff. He would swoop in to take over the reins of a troubled division, ask a million questions, and get people energized. But then he would give orders based on what *he* had done in the past, rarely implementing any new ideas or taking anyone else's advice. When he did grab an idea from someone, he never gave credit where credit was due. He came into an operation with one goal: to get promoted.

Mark's strategy was basically to dazzle a new team with illusory participation and then leave before he could be held accountable for missteps. It was only after he had moved on to another project that the staff he left behind realized that he had completely ignored everything they had said. Sometimes he left the division as success occurred, other times not, but no matter when he left, he was careful that he did not leave fingerprints on anything. His subordinates saw his stints in previous departments as the organizational equivalent of one-night stands. By the time Mark finally landed in the corner office, he had burned so many bridges that he was unable to put a team together that really wanted him to succeed. As a result, Mark was summarily fired.

If Mark had been a little smarter, he would have seen it coming. When you take over in a leadership position, you fortify your position by admitting what you don't know, asking questions, listening to those below you, and accepting—or at least acknowledging—the suggestions offered by your staff. It's all about respect: respect for the organization's history, respect for the talents and achievements of those around you, and most of all, respect for the people who will work with you to achieve your goals.

WATCH OUT FOR IMPRINTS IN THE SAND

Along with his old desk, the boss you follow has left you a legacy. It could be a mantle, or occasionally a halo. But until you establish and imprint your own mark, your predecessor's ghosts will haunt your administration.

Of course, everyone has his or her own unique profile, but we've found that most bosses fit pretty well into one of three quick-and-dirty categories:

1. The failure
2. The sinner
3. The legend

Obviously, we're painting extremes here, but learning to recognize these personalities will help you better understand how they have affected the staff you're inheriting. That, in turn, will give you some hints as to how easy or difficult it's going to be to lead people through the transition from the old regime to the new.

You might, for example, be inheriting an operation run by a leader who never hit his numbers and had little vision, or who had no social skills and couldn't manage his way out of a paper bag. Or you might be following in the footsteps of a legend, a boss revered by everyone he ever met. Most people think that replacing a weak, difficult, unsuccessful, or even unethical boss would be a slam dunk. Sometimes it works that way. Believe it or not, though, the most difficult legacy to follow is not a bad guy but a *hero*. Let's first look at what happens when you follow a boss who has been a failure.

The Failure

We believe that a failure is any boss who is a weak leader. He usually has poor management skills, exercises poor judgment, has people cover for his shortcomings, and worst of all, never makes his numbers. He rarely has a game plan and his staff is usually left wandering and wondering. What kind of scars does a failure leave on his team? First of all, because he was erratic and indecisive, your staff will in all likelihood feel hesitant and insecure. You may also inherit team members who can't give you a straight answer because they got very skilled at making excuses for your predecessor. In many cases, some members of the team have stepped into the leadership vacuum by default and are functioning above level. Some are intently focused on survival, others are dysfunctional.

If you want to keep from being blindsided, don't make the mistake of coming into a dysfunctional, poorly run organization quickly trying to impose a structure on it. In particular, those who were covering for their boss are not going to be too anxious for anyone new to take away their power. And they will resent any suddenly imposed rules—especially if none existed before.

To successfully follow a failed leader, we recommend that you:

- Applaud and acknowledge your staff's achievements, no matter how large or small. They are hungry for recognition.
- Encourage each member of the team to explain how he would improve the performance of the unit. This begins to create buy-in and, ultimately, loyalty.
- Clearly define performance expectations and incentives. Since this team has had few rewards, your approach can offer an opportunity for advancement.
- Recognize those who have been performing above level by either awarding new titles or giving them an unanticipated bonus.

The Sinner

The sinner, as you might expect, gets her reputation from being either immoral or unethical. She leads without rules, focuses on relationships over regulations, and advocates winning at any cost. Under her reign, money comes in the door, but it's probably best not to ask how.

How has the sinner affected her people? Because your new team has been working in an unstable environment, they are used to promises not kept, favored players, and squirmy deals. They are most likely tired of fighting to be heard by their boss, and they often have to duck gossip or innuendo. Their greatest fear is that they will be tarred by the boss's misdeeds, casting a reflection on their own reputations. A prime example of this took place in the athletics department of a large Midwestern university where the athletic director, who had been taking kickbacks from a vendor, had instituted a one-supplier mandate for equipment purchases. Eventually, the jig was up and the director was fired. Everyone he worked with struggled to distance themselves from him, but clearing their own names, even though they were innocent, took a long time.

When you assume leadership after a sinner, take a big, deep breath before you start slamming the guy who came before you. Hashing over the sins of the past reopens old wounds and prolongs the healing process. Don't pretend to be a white knight who has arrived to redeem the operation. All you will do is further alienate your staff and make it harder for you to shift the culture.

So how do you successfully follow the sinner and establish a new imprint? We recommend that you:

- Quickly establish your credentials and beliefs. Once your staff has a clear picture of what you deem acceptable behavior and performance, and how you want to conduct business, they can either follow you or ask to move on.
- Acknowledge errant past practices. This will create an atmosphere of candor and encourage less secrecy.
- Lead with empathy. The team has never had this kind of leadership, and an empathetic leader can create an atmosphere of integrity and honesty that did not exist in the department before.

The Legend

Legends command unquestionable loyalty and devotion. They can take a company to new levels of success and performance. Some are extremely charismatic like Jack Welch, some more reserved like Bill Gates, others more controversial like Martha Stewart. Whatever their personality, legends always have a clearly defined management style and an amazing history of unparalleled success.

So how do you follow a legend and still leave your own mark? This was the challenge for Sam Palmisano, who succeeded Lou Gerstner as CEO of IBM. During his nine-year reign, Gerstner had changed the corporation's core focus and almost single-handedly saved IBM from self-destructing. In his book *Who Says Elephants Can't Dance?* Gerstner offers a personal account of how he revitalized IBM's business and culture and increased profits by 40 percent.[3]

Sam Palmisano had the bad luck to take the helm from the legendary Gerstner just as the dot-com balloon was starting to lose air. He also came in with a totally different personal management style. One senior exec described Gerstner as charming and "a leader we would follow to the ends of the earth," but also as somewhat formal, brusque, and at times intimidating. Palmisano, on the other hand, is a warm, personable, and approachable leader who immediately wins over just about everyone he meets, customers and employees alike. People inside and outside the company feel relaxed and comfortable enough around him to always call him "Sam."

Taking over IBM at the start of the worst tech tumble in history, Palmisano needed a radical solution. Gerstner had already set a precedent by dramatically shifting the culture and climate of the company. And that set the stage for Palmisano to do the same—which is exactly what he did. He chose to establish and push a new business model that positioned IBM as the company to which other corporations could outsource their operations. It was more than simply taking over data centers, which IBM had been doing for more than a decade. IBM now handles after-sales product support for everyone from Cisco to Philips Consumer Electronics. Currently, over 20 percent of IBM's $5.1 billion research and development budget is devoted to services-related research. It is returning IBM to its once predominant role in the tech industry.

Palmisano's success is a result of three key decisions he made in assuming the leadership from a legend. The template he created can be used by any new leader—regardless of the size of the company—who finds himself stepping into a legend's shoes.

1. He maintained his own personal management style and didn't try to co-opt Gerstner's.
2. He set his own course for the company based on current market conditions and the competitive situation. He wasn't swayed by any past history of glory.
3. He insisted on challenging the "Lou always did it this way" current that ran through the company.

To sum it up, even though every boss you follow will have a lasting impact on your staff, the only way you can succeed is to do your homework and understand the legacy you're inheriting. This knowledge will guide you, as a new leader, in those heady first days as you stand in front of your staff and decide how you can most effectively get everyone marching in the same direction. It may very well be the difference between an easy transition and a rocky one. Most important, doing your homework will prevent you from being blindsided.

Take a Good Look in the Mirror: Are You the Kind of Manager You Think You Are?

Most successful leaders view themselves as intense, committed, and driven. But their staff often has a completely different view, and may interpret that "intense, committed, driven" manager's style as arrogant, domineering, more terrifying than motivating, more intimidating than inspiring, more frustrating than supportive.

Many leaders try to maintain a good sense of themselves through a protective mechanism called *self-justifying image*. Leaders use this self-protective mechanism not only to justify their behavior, but also to preemptively defend themselves against attack, according to the Arbinger Institute's study entitled *Leadership and Self-Deception*.* Simply put, these leaders convince themselves that certain behaviors are acceptable, even while employees find those same behaviors intolerable.

In our decades in the trenches, we have worked with—and continue to see—four types of managers who are, in essence, in complete denial, totally clueless about the negative impact they are having on their employees.

- The *toxic* manager bases his decisions on his street smarts. He can't fully explain the rationale behind his decisions or give employees the details they need to execute the plan. A toxic manager says that he just feels this is the right way to go and then launches into

*Arbinger Institute, *Leadership and Self-Deception* (San Francisco: Berrett Publishers, 2000).

unrelated stories of past successes. As a result, everyone gets extremely frustrated. True toxic managers rarely see that *they* are the real problem, and they even more rarely have an "aha" moment about why everything around them is collapsing. The only time they may wake up is after missing their numbers three quarters in a row, which forces them to spend an inordinate amount of time making excuses for their lackluster performance.

- Check out the *VISA man,* an investment banker in Chicago. His staff came up with this label—behind his back, of course—because they saw him as someone who managed to *take credit* for everything. In the process, he managed to kill any chance for loyalty among his team.

- The *Teflon man* is a true manipulator. Why Teflon? Because nothing ever sticks to the guy. When things hit the fan and the missiles are zinging, he *always* manages to find a scapegoat. Under his reign, the turnover can be rampant.

- The *Good Humor Man* is a compassionate soul who tries to make everyone happy and leads by always forgiving bad behavior or poor performance. His staff sees a leader whose judgment is flawed, and whose forgiving nature actually compromises the entire operation and put the team's efforts at risk.

The point of all this? Simple. If you think you're a great manager, get some perspective. Look around and listen to others. What you hear from them may very well surprise you.

HAVE YOU BEEN CHOSEN OVER YOUR PEERS?

Getting promoted out of the ranks is essentially a victory, whether you think of it in those terms or not. The fact is that you were competing with a colleague and you won. And now one or more people you used to work with side-by-side may be reporting to you. Whether your new staff and former peers become your allies or your adversaries is completely up to you. As you can imagine, this is a situation rife with I-didn't-see-it-coming moments.

If you're in this situation, it's essential that you remember that your relationship with the people you used to work with has changed. As hard as it may be for everyone involved, the reality is that you're not in the clubhouse anymore and you're going to have to resist the temptation to behave like you're still part of the old gang. Feel free to have an occasional lunch with your former work buddies, but be prepared to draw some clear boundaries.

As the new leader, you want—and deserve—respect, commitment, and strong performance. If you think the best way to achieve this is to get everyone to like you, think again. *Being liked is not your first priority*. If your staff respects you and believes that you value their contribution, they *will* work hard.

Mary Chakowski's story is a perfect example of someone who didn't appreciate the perils of being promoted from the ranks and got completely blindsided. Mary and her colleague Bob Turner worked for a major New York advertising agency and reported to senior VP Joe O'Hare. Although Joe had been with the agency for years, his lack of leadership was jeopardizing the agency's biggest account. Mary and Bob decided to take a risky step and brought the problem to the CEO, whose response was to fire Joe and move Mary into the senior VP slot, effectively promoting her over Bob. Still, Mary asked Bob to stay on as an integral part of her team, and their business relationship continued as usual, with frequent conferences about staff, budgets, and creativity.

Just a few weeks into her new position, Mary was called to a meeting with the senior VP of human resources and the agency's general counsel. Much to her astonishment, Mary was confronted with the news that Bob had filed a sexual harassment claim against her. He had cited the many dinners, confidences, and late-night calls as examples of harassment. Mary countered with a strong defense. Her staff was questioned, and Bob's claim lost its credibility. But the trust between Mary and Bob was shattered and Mary was left with the unpleasant task of asking Bob to leave the company.

It took Mary several months to solidify control of her team after this costly distraction. Given that Mary's mistake is very common among first-time managers, take her story as a cautionary tale.

From a broader perspective, the combination of hurt feelings, bruised egos, disappointed psyches, and a little unbridled ambition, can do strange things to former equals who suddenly find themselves in a boss/subordinate relationship. Watch out for those who refuse to get with the program so you don't get blindsided. If anyone on your team—whether it's a new member or a former peer—can't support your transition to boss, you may have to cut her loose.

LOOKING THE PART

We really wish this weren't the case, but even though we're sure you got your recent promotion because of your unique combination of skills and talents, some of your ability to succeed in your new job will depend on how you look. Bottom line: Your title sends a message, but so does everything you say, wear, and write.

Do you like what you see in the mirror? Do you need to change it? Is it creating the impression you want to create? Do you need to learn how to give an articulate presentation? Do you need some lessons in social skills or table manners? Do you need an executive coach? With *every* upward step, you need to upgrade your look and manner. We're talking your watch, your shoes, your haircut, your vocabulary, and maybe even your choice of beverage. After all, ordering a 20-year-old single malt scotch or a glass of Sancerre says "I'm the boss" a lot louder than "Gimme a Bud Lite" or a froufrou drink with an umbrella.

While it's important to establish yourself as the boss in the eyes of the people who work for you, the higher you go, it's even more important to play to the crowd *above* you. The old adage about dressing for the next level up the ladder still holds true. If you look successful, people will believe that you are. Call them shallow, but that's the way it is. Industrial psychologist Edgar Schein noted in his research on social influence that the way we dress and our social manners communicate to others who we are.[4] As you climb the corporate ladder, those subtle messages become even more critical.

Like you, your peers are trying to catch the eye of senior management. They know that their future progress hinges on being seen as a leader and an influential player.

As the generals walk down the line, reviewing the troops, be sure your crew is spiffy, your dress blues are pressed, and your shoes and brass are polished to a shine that reflects the confident leader you are.

CHAPTER 2   Takeaways

1. Accept congratulations with humility and grace when you become the new leader.
2. Create a climate of candor, clarity, and credibility.
3. Define your management style and know how it impacts others.
4. Remember to say "I don't know," because new leaders don't need to have all the answers.
5. When you pose questions, be sure to *really* listen to the answers.
6. Do your homework: Learn about the leader who came before you.
7. Focus on being respected, not liked.
8. Look the part, act the part, walk the walk. It all counts!

3

The House of Mirrors, or How to Keep Your Perspective

Remember those funhouses at the carnival? The ones where you walk through the door and are immediately surrounded by mirrors that distort your image? In one mirror you're skinny; in another, short. Or tall. Or fat. It's hard to gauge your distance without bumping into things, and you can't always be sure which way to go and which route is the safest. In short, nothing is what it appears to be.

So, too, in the world of business. When you take over the corner office you gain power over other people—control not only over your employees' reviews, promotions, titles, and salaries, but over the very way they see themselves. This power alters how you see yourself and how you see the world.

Every year at the Four Seasons Hotel in Chicago, a large, well-known insurance company hosts its annual holiday party. Last year's party was hosted by the new company president, Peter Moore. Surrounded by his inner circle and other members of the executive team, Peter was holding court in a corner of the Michigan Room, regaling the troops with stories of his past successes in the industry. His audience seemed to hang on his every word and laughter filled the room. Peter's wife, Theresa, watched from across the room and the second she finally caught Peter's eye, she tapped her wrist, sending a familiar signal that it was time to go. Peter reluctantly excused himself from the group and made his way to Theresa's side.

Noticeably annoyed, Peter whispered to Theresa, "We can't leave now. They love me. They're laughing at my stories. It's important that they get to know me as a person." Theresa, having been a savvy corporate wife for over 20 years, whispered back, "You just don't get it, Peter! You're the boss, and no one is really going to have a good time at this party until *you* leave."

Employees surrounding you at a party, laughing at your jokes, smiling at your stories, and making you feel like the king of the jungle are doing exactly what employees do best: playing to the power. For that reason, the last time you'll ever hear completely honest and undistorted information about what's going on in your company is the day *before* you start arranging those pictures of your family on your new desk. This is a tremendously important point, so you might want to go back and read that sentence again.

Most executives approach the corner office with good intentions: They want to lead effectively, be fair, articulate goals, and motivate their employees to follow them up any hill. But too many get blindsided along the way because they lose perspective. So from this point forward, the biggest challenge you face is to maintain your perspective—about your power, your impact on your employees, the way you are seen by others, and the influence you wield.

SIZING UP THE TEAM

Managing personnel—hiring, training, motivating, evaluating, and even firing employees—is a critical issue for managers. When you get put into a position of authority, senior management will judge you by the strength of the team you put together, not just your own personal performance. The most successful and powerful leaders surround themselves with talented, strong, decisive, skilled, and outspoken players.

Some staffs you inherit; others you build. Whatever form your team takes, you should strategically evaluate the qualifications and talents you need to accomplish specific jobs and goals. The sooner you determine who's getting the job done, who works better in which positions, the more quickly you'll be able to analyze and define your team profile. The next step, if the budget allows, is to begin the process of adding the new talent you need to round out a winning roster. A solidly constructed team affords you the best shot at managing effectively and, therefore, achieving your goals. We're going to pretty much steer clear of all that, because this isn't a book on the basics of management, and there are already many excellent books on the topic. Instead, what we focus on in this chapter is how to spot and avoid potential personnel problems before they derail *your* career.

Evaluating the Bench

Let's start by taking a look at the team you've just inherited. You may already have at your fingertips all the facts you need about everyone on your team: work history, commission statements, performance evaluations, and other important pieces of information. But when it comes down to deciding who stays on the team and who doesn't, you'll need to rely in large measure on your wisdom and experience. You don't want to make many changes too quickly, but here are a number of critical questions you should ask yourself about every single member of your team:

- If I set a standard of high achievement, will this person meet the challenge?
- Does this person share the drive and excitement with others on the team?
- Does this person have the ability and talent to stretch and hit the higher waterline?
- How is this person going to respond to changes in approach, attitude, and atmosphere?
- Will this person ramp up and get it?
- Does this person fit the culture shift I am establishing for us to win?
- Will this person be able to work effectively with the rest of the team regardless of new promotions and the like?

Hiring Land Mines

There are two major traps new bosses often fall into when they start to assemble their teams. One is hiring weak staff members. The other is violating the cultural ethos of the company.

Surrounding oneself with weak subordinates may sound like a dumb thing to do, and it is. But that hasn't stopped a lot of managers from doing it. The reality is that your less-than-stellar staff members reflect poorly on you and raise questions with senior management about your ability and judgment. Weak employees will never challenge you, never give you honest feedback, never take risks, and can never be relied on to improve the team's performance. On the other hand, when you hire strong people, talented in areas where you lack expertise, you add a fuller complement of skills to the team, you get honest debate, and your very capable team will drive the business forward. Management will surely take note that you have surrounded yourself with winners.

Too many executives overlook their organization's culture when hiring subordinates. Big mistake. An organization's culture is its ethos—its look, its rhythm, its customs, its value system, its way of doing business. Talent and credentials are important, but so is *fit*—making sure that the prospective team member would mesh with your particular organization, style of management, business, and other team members. If you don't acknowledge the importance of culture, how

(Continued)

51

can you possibly bring in a member of the team who will fit in? We have seen many cases where a manager hired a brilliant but quirky employee, brought him into a conservative company, and then watched it blow up because it just wasn't a good fit. It's all about style and values, and the higher one moves within an organization, the more fit becomes a determinant of success.

Round Out the Roster

Finding talented people with the right mix of talents and company fit is key to a winning effort. And sometimes, of course, you'll need to go outside your organization to fill gaps. As we said earlier, there's no shortage of information out there on how to screen and hire employees. Being a smart interviewer will allow you to quickly and efficiently solicit the strategic information you need to make your decisions. But there's one area of the hiring process that is too often overlooked by managers, sometimes with appalling consequences: checking references.

Having hired and fired hundreds of employees and talked to managers who have hired hundreds more, we have adopted three questions from a search consultant we respect. We suggest that all executives use them during the reference checking process, long before making an offer to a candidate. These questions encourage candid conversation about your candidate, are legally permissible, and give you a clearer picture, beyond the usual descriptors, of the person's potential.

1. If I hire this candidate, what will surprise me about her after the first three months?
2. What would this candidate have to do to be top of her class?
3. If we were to create the ideal job for this candidate, what would that job look like?

Birthdays Matter

Small things matter. They signal appreciation and acknowledgment of an employee's worth. When Amy Kopelan ran *Episodes* magazine, she started what became a staff tradition—impromptu celebrations for each team member's birthday or anniversary at the company. The small hoopla acknowledged that each employee mattered. It kept the troops engaged, pumped up, and committed, and it encouraged performance. Jack Welch, an icon of American management, nurtured top talent by delivering praise with a flurry of handwritten notes and bottles of champagne, saying "job well done." Nancy Widmann, as president of CBS Radio, always sent house plants and flowers to spouses of transferred executives, welcoming them to their new city. These are simple, quick gestures that are so easy to do and are talked about for weeks.

The Unwritten Contract

At the heart of every boss–employee relationship there is a set of assumed rules. This isn't an actual document that gets signed, and it's not even part of a standard employment contract. Nevertheless, every leader and every employee understands it on an *unspoken level*. These rules—call them an unwritten contract—imply *mutual* respect and *shared responsibility*. If one or the other gives way, the relationship is in danger of crumbling. This unwritten contract is the fundamental structure upon which you can lead and succeed, or from which you can inadvertently stumble into an I-didn't-see-it-coming pit. The balance is extremely delicate, and it's up to you to make sure it doesn't get too overloaded in either direction.

OVERSTEPPING BOUNDARIES

The wall poster says, "It is lonely at the top." One of the challenges, therefore, for a new manager is to keep perspective when he faces isolation in the corner office. As a leader, you know that setting boundaries between you and your staff is important, but living with the boundary can be difficult. To offset it, leaders and managers come to rely on a smaller and smaller circle of people for advice and counsel, but this is not without peril. It causes you to lose perspective because you are no longer getting an unfiltered view. Your input has narrowed. The result can often be an unclear picture. This "ivory tower" conundrum can also bring about flawed judgment regarding the relationships you rely on and those in whom you confide.

Both seasoned and first-time managers make the mistake of choosing a staff member to serve as confidante. This is a risky proposition, although it seems harmless—even intuitive—on the face of it. Why does it initially feel right? As a manager, you are happy to find someone who will listen unconditionally, offer confirmation of your genius, pose no tough questions, and, for the most part, pose no challenge. As this relationship develops, it becomes harder and harder for you to assess your confidante's talents, you become myopic as to this employee's real value, and you get a slanted perspective of the contributions from the rest of your team.

Let's see how a too-close-for-comfort relationship backfired at a large pharmaceutical company. Cleo Hyatt was a senior VP and her first in command was Shelly Klein. Shelly had been working for Cleo for more than five years and in that time had become a close confidante. Cleo shared with Shelly how anxious she was about an upcoming three-day, off-site meeting at a resort in California. It was a major event for Cleo and her division. More than 100 staff members would meet to attend seminars, meetings, dinners, and social festivities. Senior management was always invited. Months in advance of the conference, formal invitations were sent out, speakers were confirmed, menus planned, and executive suites booked. Cleo agonized over every detail with Shelly, stressing how important it was that the event be a success, and worrying out loud about the terrible things that would happen if the event didn't work out as planned.

Three weeks before the event, Cleo's assistant, Ellen Smythe, called the resort's catering director to review final arrangements. Ellen was stunned when the director told her that the event had been cancelled—by Cleo herself—a few days before. He had given the dates away to another company. Panicked, Ellen took the news to Cleo. Cleo, knowing how critical it was to salvage what she could, immediately jumped on the phone, spoke to the resort's general manager, and was able to rebook her event for the following month. Memos went out to everyone, and all was changed successfully.

The situation was clearly embarrassing for Cleo, but not career ending. A post-mortem investigation into what had *really* happened pointed to Cleo's trusted confidante, Shelly Klein, as the faux Cleo who had cancelled the event. Tired of waiting for Cleo to move on, jealous of her career success, and armed with all the insider knowledge she needed, Shelly had plotted what she hoped would be Cleo's demise. It was a major blindside and a classic tale of not seeing it coming.

In a similar twist, Elaine Eisenman recently consulted for a national retailer in New York City. Maggie, one of the marketing VPs Elaine worked with, confided that she was getting a huge amount of unsolicited attention from headhunters. What Maggie didn't know was that one of her division marketing managers, soured by what he felt was an unfair performance review, had posted Maggie's resume on a number of job hunting web sites, hoping to cause trouble and remove her from his chain of command.

Of course, not all insider confidantes fall into the *caveat emptor* category, but in most cases choosing someone from your team is unwise. The chance of being blindsided is too great. A far better course of action is to put together a *team* of confidantes from outside the company—the personal board of directors we referred to in Chapter 1: colleagues you trust from various industries, experienced players from outside your division, and valued members of your family.

The staff confidante is not the only subordinate you may be tempted to nestle under your leadership wing. You might also develop a close relationship with a talented up-and-comer who you think has potential. But watch out. It's incredibly easy to get caught up in the role of mentor or coach and lose your perspective. Here's an example of how missing the cues undermined one manager's authority and jeopardized his business objectives.

Rory Mitchell was president of Jefford Partners, a leader in the legal executive search field in Atlanta. Six search consultants and two support staff worked at Jefford. Deciding to grow the firm, Mitchell hired a young high-potential lawyer, Larry Perrone, to come on board as a new search associate. Perrone had spent six years with a large law firm in Dallas, had some good contacts in the Atlanta legal community, and was anxious to make a career change. Mitchell thought he would be a great candidate.

Perrone proved to be a quick study. He ingratiated himself with most of the senior search consultants but drew particular attention from Rory, whom he sought out for guidance, coaching, and industry knowledge. Mitchell loved Perrone's energy, drive, and enthusiasm for tough assignments. Pegging him as the firm's next superstar, Mitchell spent more and more time coaching Perrone, taking him along on client calls and introducing him to key contacts within the Atlanta legal community.

What Mitchell didn't know was that others in the firm weren't nearly as excited about Perrone and thought he was manipulating Mitchell. Mitchell ignored the rumors and offered Perrone a two-year employment contract. But instead of accepting the job, Perrone tendered his resignation and announced that he was starting his own business—and taking one of Jefford's longtime support staff with him. Mitchell's huge investment in time, energy, and resources had been completely wasted. Even worse, he had inadvertently created a viable competitor.

How did a really savvy leader like Mitchell let his mentoring relationship get so far off course? Ultimately, his vision had been obscured by the warm and fuzzy feeling that so many senior leaders get when they're being flattered by young up-and-comers who often remind them of themselves. Staying alert to the signs that a mentoring relationship has become unbalanced is the key to protecting yourself from being blindsided. Here are three red flags to watch for:

1. You have different rules for your mentee than for the rest of your staff.
2. You are spending more time coaching your mentee than growing your business.
3. You ignore sound advice and quiet comments from colleagues about the expanding role your mentee is assuming inside the company.

THE UNANTICIPATED PITFALL

As important as it is to keep your perspective when it comes to managing your employees, be aware that unpleasant surprises can come from places where you'd least expect them: the floor above.

In many cases it starts with something as innocuous as a call from the C-suite that goes like this: "There is someone in my office that I want you to meet." When you hear something like that, be very careful and very vigilant. "There's someone I want you to meet" is often the opening salvo in senior management's attempt to get you to take someone into your operation. This could be:

- A son, daughter, or other relative of the CEO.
- A difficult and protected employee.
- A college roommate's daughter or son.
- A personal connection from the golf or yacht club.
- A potential or former girlfriend/boyfriend.
- An ex-boss or ex-boss's boss who has only a few years until retirement and no one has the guts to let them go.

In the best-case scenario, your new staffer could turn out to be brilliant, unassuming, and hardworking. He could tell senior management that you're amazingly talented, a great leader, working too hard, and very underpaid. Or he could sprout wings and cluck like a chicken. The chances are about the same.

Here's a somewhat more realistic scenario. Your new employee will feel unbelievably entitled. If he begins to fail, he'll blame it on you and/or your lack of guidance and leadership. He'll point out where you have helped others but not him. You'll quickly find yourself waist-deep in a serious personnel problem with no one around to back you up. This blindside doesn't have to happen.

Consider Susan Brown's story. As senior VP of human resources at Full Essentials, a well-known retail chain in the Midwest specializing in clothes for large-size women, Brown was in the unenviable position of working for a company that was going gangbusters, but not having the budget to hire the staff necessary to handle the growth. One morning, the company's president called Susan to say that he had a good friend, Lorna Aston, who had just retired and was looking for contract work. If he put Aston on his budget, would Brown be interested in using her services? Sounded like a win-win to Susan. Her boss clearly recognized her staffing challenges and seemed to be genuinely trying to help Susan and her division.

Aston joined Brown's team two weeks later and the first words out of her mouth were, "I'm here to direct. I don't source, and I don't make phone calls. Your people will do that and I will create charts and progress reports." All of a sudden Susan wasn't feeling nearly as optimistic. She had a feeling that trouble was brewing, but kept it to herself.

Almost immediately, Susan started getting calls from peers asking, "Who is Lorna Aston?" and reporting regular Lorna sightings in the president's office. Soon Susan was getting calls and e-mails from the president himself, questioning her every management decision. She started spending more of her time defending herself and less time doing what she was supposed to do: manage her department. Susan suspected that this was all about Lorna, yet she couldn't prove it. Realizing that the CEO was losing faith in her, and worried that she was going to be fired, Susan decided to resign.

Had Susan had her eyes open from the beginning and known how to recognize the signs, she might still have her job. To start with, she should have smelled trouble when the president offered to help her with her staffing issues— on his nickel! Flags don't get much bigger or much redder than that. Every savvy executive knows that senior management doesn't increase your head count just to be nice. The *only* time the CEO calls out of the blue and sends you someone is when he needs a favor. Second, as Lorna's assurance and bravado were growing, it was a clear indication that a control shift was taking place and Susan's power was being threatened. Here are the steps she should have taken to manage this difficult situation:

- *Gather intelligence.* Who is the new person? How is she connected to your boss? Raise your antenna fully.
- *Pose a strategic question to the boss.* What does senior management really want to happen? Figure out how much flexibility you have.
- *Create a paper trail.* Hang up the phone and start writing! Start a file of memos, e-mails, questions, reports, and evaluations.
- *Have a "Come to Jesus" meeting with your new subordinate.* Try to clear the air and ask what you can do to make this work.
- *When all else fails, consider relocating the new hire to one of your peers.* Call it a promotion or do whatever else it takes. Hey, this is guerilla warfare.

OUT OF SIGHT SHOULD *NEVER* MEAN OUT OF MIND

Since some of your employees may not work in the same building or even city as you do, it's essential that you maintain your vigilance over everyone who reports to you, whether you see them every day or once a year.

Lois Packard is an example of an otherwise solid leader who misjudged an experienced manager in an outside office and got blindsided. Lois was general counsel of a regional construction firm based just outside of Albany, New

York, and oversaw all the lawyers in the company, including those at the Montreal operation.

Because the Canadian office was responsible for various important local filings that differed from those in the United States, Packard had weekly status calls with Martine Bouchard, the lead attorney in the Montreal office. Bouchard had been with the firm for many years and, because Packard trusted Bouchard's judgment and expertise, she rarely visited the office. She was relieved that she could focus on the lawyers in Albany and delegate full responsibility for Montreal to Bouchard.

But when Bouchard was in a serious accident and needed time off for rehab, Packard was forced to become involved. She hired a temporary lawyer to fill in during Bouchard's leave. Less than a week into the job, the temp called Packard with some sobering news. He had discovered piles of un-filed legal documents on Bouchard's desk, along with letters requiring late fees for missed filings and a large number of default warnings.

Packard flew to Montreal immediately. Once on-site, it didn't take long for her to discover that everyone at the Montreal office knew about Bouchard's irregular and haphazard work pattern, but they were afraid to alert Packard. They all assumed that on some level she knew, and because nothing changed, they also assumed that Packard wasn't concerned. Wrong! Packard had to scramble fast to rescue her company from serious legal problems. In the end, she did, but because the office was her responsibility, *her* job with the company, not just Bouchard's, was in jeopardy.

How could Packard have avoided a blindsiding situation? Her mistake was getting too comfortable and losing perspective. She trusted a senior, experienced manager to run an outside operation and never took the time to be on-site to audit the operation. Bottom line: If you're not on the premises and don't visit often enough to develop close, personal relationships with people in that location, you'll never be able to understand the dynamics and catch a problem. It is *always* necessary to be visible and accessible to every area of your responsibility. This is important whether you have a new manager or a company pro running an operation. Circumstances change, people change, business pressures change, and you must stay on top of it all.

When you have global responsibility for a geographically distributed work force, it's good business—and a vital self-preservation tactic—to stay tuned into everything that's happening. Sometimes the rules make it easier. A good example is a U.S. banking law that requires all employees to take two consecutive weeks of vacation. The rationale is that a two-week absence should offer a long enough window to determine whether the employee is engaged in any type of illegal activity. Are there other methods you can use to detect trouble in your outside offices? Absolutely. They all require vigilance and ongoing oversight. We suggest the following:

Out-of-Sight Oversight

- Ask for five years' worth of numbers from your outside offices. Pore over them. Patterns will emerge. Watch out for unusual expenses, complex trade deals, or profit spikes.
- Investigate unusual turnover with the support staff. It bodes trouble.
- Pay attention when you have difficulty hiring in the local market. Is the company's reputation in that city a problem?

- Review transfer requests. Are too many people asking to leave? Are too many people trying to transfer in?
- During site visits, meet with every person individually to ask, "How's it going?" Be sure that everyone sees you as approachable and open. This is not easy but keep at it.
- Watch how often your manager defers to staff for answers. The lack of knowledge might suggest that the manager isn't really in charge or aware.
- Do an honest gut check. Do you detect any uneasiness in the room?
- Don't postpone on-site visits at the request of your manager, and don't always give advance notice that you're coming in. Just show up!

ONE MORE LOOK IN THE MIRROR

Seeing a true picture of yourself, your situation, and your relationship with employees is one of the biggest challenges to making it through the funhouse of self-deception. To uncloud the mirror, be aware of your own biases in dealing with staff, be sure that the adulation of subordinates doesn't fog up the image before you, and be objective and discerning in listening to information presented to you. What are people filtering out? What are they filtering in?

Never stop looking in the mirror, but make sure it's an undistorted one. Loss of perspective is still one of the greatest land mines you can trip over and one of the most dangerous leadership vulnerabilities. Remember the unwritten contract you have with your subordinates. As an enlightened leader, you must create an environment that invites high morale, low turnover, consistently peak performance, and a reputation for integrity and fairness. It won't take long for senior management to get the message. Don't lose your perspective. Narcissus is a perfect image to keep in mind. The handsome Greek youth was so taken by his own image reflected in the mirrored surface of a still pond that he lay on the bank and slowly pined away, staring into the water.

CHAPTER 3 Takeaways

1. When you're promoted to a management role, concentrate on keeping perspective.
2. Honor the boss-employee unwritten contract of mutual respect.
3. Unearth the truth about your style and how others see you.
4. Find small ways to signal appreciation for your employees' efforts.
5. Get advice from a personal board of directors, not a confidante from your staff.
6. Set boundaries when you mentor a person on the team.
7. Call a "Come to Jesus" meeting when all else fails.
8. When you manage outside offices, show up on-site unannounced.

4

COMRADES, COALITIONS, AND COMPETITORS

No matter how talented, educated, qualified, beautiful, or charming you are, you'll never be able to get where you want to go in your company without, to paraphrase the Beatles, "a little help from your colleagues." Whether you're looking for power, access, visibility, a promotion, or some combination of these, you'll have a far better chance of achieving your goals if you have the right connections and you've made the right alliances. Over the years, we've seen colleagues form networks of ambitious and trusted peers who act as sounding boards for each other, provide valuable reconnaissance and inside information, and help each other weather all kinds of crises. On the most fundamental level, you're seeking to create a *personal trade agreement*, an alliance of influential peers who have agreed to work together for each other's mutual benefit and to help each other "see it coming."

YOUR OWN BAND OF BROTHERS OR SISTERS OR SIBLINGS OR . . .

Early in our careers, the three of us recognized the need for a band of brothers. Under the best of circumstances, these bands become a *fellowship of ambition* on the organizational landscape. Here's an example. Some years back, there were a number of very talented, ambitious, motivated producers at ABC Sports. They formed a coalition that basically said, "I have your back." The understanding was:

- We support each other inside and outside the company.
- We never do anything to discredit each other.
- When one of us moves up, we take the others along.

Although this kind of alliance and coalition has been more traditionally exercised by male colleagues, we are seeing more bands of sisters form inside of organizations as women shift from being competitive with each other to being more collaborative, especially as they move higher in their organizations.

But whether you're male or female, if you don't put together personal trade agreements with influential people, you run the risk of being blindsided by someone else who has a stronger agreement in place. That's exactly what happened to our colleague Hannah Sedi.

Baking Bread Basics was one of the newest and most successful shows on a food cable channel. Hannah was a segment editor for *Baking Bread Basics* as well as another food show, *The Weekend Brunch*. Things were going so well with *Bread* that the show's producers let people know they were looking to staff up and hire an assistant producer. Since these jobs came up rarely, it was a coveted opportunity. Following company procedure, Hannah submitted her resume, was called in for an interview, and was recommended for the promotion by several other editors. Hannah heard from inside sources that she had a far better chance of getting the position than most of the other candidates.

A few days after the interviewing process had closed, one of the producers told Hannah that she wasn't going to get the assistant producer job. Instead, it was going to Elizabeth Wong, a production assistant from another show. Elizabeth had been a last-minute entry in the interviewing process, and a surprise winner. But it just so happened that Elizabeth's graphic designer on her show, one of her band of sisters, knew the hiring producer and made a call on Elizabeth's behalf. Favors were called in, the trade agreement went into effect, and Elizabeth ordered new business cards.

Trade agreements are really about *connection politics*. And Hannah simply hadn't leveraged her coalition as effectively as Elizabeth had.

Reciprocity

Trade agreements among colleagues work *only* when there is reciprocity. While there's definitely a you-scratch-my-back-and-I'll-scratch-yours quality to it, reciprocity isn't about keeping score or matching favor for favor. It's more about living up to the expectation that you'll help another colleague as much as he or she will help you. It's about alerting someone about a management change, making the phone call to help someone land a position, or giving someone a heads-up about an opening. Reciprocity is what gives trade agreements their strength. Without it they'd fall apart completely.

Striking Up the Band

When talking with clients about the importance of the band of brothers, we often hear a lot of questions. How do you set it up? How do you know whom to trust? How many people should be in the band? How do you approach them? Is the trade agreement written? What if one person is always asking for favors but never seems to help anyone else?

 As you might guess, the answers to almost all of these questions begin with, "Well, it depends . . ." However, there are a few very important guidelines.

- *Start slowly.* If you're young and just starting off in your career, or you're beginning a new job with a company, understand that it may take a while before you can identify prospective comrades. The more senior you are, the more people you'll know—both inside and outside your organization—and the better your instincts will be. Putting together your band of colleagues is a long-term process.

- *Let it happen.* The ABC Sports producers aside, most trade agreements are completely informal and just sort of happen. There's no written contract and, in most cases, no unwritten one, either. People somehow find each other. The rules aren't spelled out; everyone who's in instinctively knows what's expected. While there's really nothing that can make an informal agreement stick, it's a good idea to create the infamous paper trail. Send a quick, informal e-mail memorializing the situation. Something like, "Lisa, great to talk with you. I'm delighted that we decided to work together on this project." Or even a "Thanks for the advice" note. These subtle examples serve as reminders to the troops that there's a trade agreement in place.

- *Watch for signs.* Say you're in sales and you're out sick for a couple of days. A coworker steps in, covers your list for you, and keeps your accounts happy. Or someone from another department gives you a heads-up that you're about to be downsized or that there's a great job opening up that you should apply for. You've just identified a couple of good trade partners. Overall, you're looking for people who are loyal, talented, who applaud and support you, who are respected in the organization.

- *Hold up your end of the deal.* If you don't feel the need to reciprocate when someone does you a good turn, you'll never be able to leverage the benefits of the alliance.

- *Know when to fire someone.* Even though your band won't have a formal agreement or a set of written rules, you may need to get rid of the deadwood, people who just aren't going along with the program. If this happens, you might need to pull someone aside and say something like, "We're all trying to help each other out here, but it feels like you're not holding up your end of the deal."

(Continued)

- *Keep it small.* If you're fairly junior, two to three people in your band is plenty. Increase that number as you get more senior, but try to keep the total under six or seven.

- *Keep your expectations reasonable.* Your trade partners don't have to be friends or even people you socialize with. They just have to be people you respect, you want to support, and who want to do the same for you. Always remember that there's a big difference between socializing and friendship. Do whatever it takes to develop a trust relationship, but at the same time, make sure that friendship doesn't get in the way of what is essentially an agreement of mutual support. Friendship is an added benefit, but be certain to keep emotional entanglements at bay.

- *Don't burn bridges.* Understand that someone who's in your band might leave your company. While that person would no longer be in the insider group, having a contact who works for a competitor and who has access to industry information could be very beneficial to you in the long run. As your career grows, you may find that your band of brothers will expand across several businesses—all positive connections for you.

One of our former colleagues, Louise Simpson, understood the importance of reciprocity. When her daughter was seeking an internship with a large ad firm in New York, Louise phoned one of her fellow board members who knew the ad firm president and asked him to arrange an introduction for her daughter. He did, and Louise's daughter landed the summer internship. Six months later, Louise picked up some information that her friend from the board was up for a major new position at her company and she went out of her way to promote his candidacy. That's reciprocity in action.

Reality Check

When Ed Koch was mayor of New York City, he was famous for walking around the city and asking people, "How am I doing?" Voters tend to answer that kind of question every four years at the polls. But Koch understood that he could run the city more effectively if he listened to problems and responded to his constituents every day.

It's very much the same in a corporate setting except that you're running for reelection a lot more frequently than the mayor of New York City. You probably get an annual performance review from your boss and, maybe, some "attaboy's" on occasion. But let's face it—the feedback you get in an annual review comes too late for you to make many substantive changes to save your year.

What you need is a reality check—honest, day in, day out input from people you can trust—not only about your performance, but also about how you're perceived. You can't just go around poking your head into people's offices and ask them out of the blue how you're doing. Okay, you could, but you'd get a lot of funny looks. So what can you do? Simple: Tap into your band of brothers or sisters. The reality check is most effective when it comes from a colleague who is striving as hard as you and who really knows what is at stake—someone who is as invested in you as you are in them.

If your presentation didn't rock the room, you need her to be honest with you. If the last person you hired is causing friction in the department, you need her to clue you in. If your jokes at client dinners consistently fizzle, you need her to call you out on it. Conversely, if you shoot the lights out and wow senior management, you'll want a colleague who will applaud!

Stephen Hassan was a senior manager at a large Midwestern manufacturing firm. A new VP was coming on board and Stephen had been tapped by the CEO to announce the new boss's arrival at a companywide staff meeting. This wasn't going to be easy, because the new boss was known in the industry as a serious cost cutter and was famous for being very difficult to work with. None of the staff knew who the new guy was, and not knowing who was going to be moving into that empty office had made them anxious, apprehensive, and worried about job security.

Stephen was in a tough spot. There was a lot coming down the pike that he couldn't talk about. Still, he had to reassure the staff as much as possible and give them some insight into the new boss's work ethic so they could pick up some clues to help increase their chances of surviving the tough road ahead. Oh, and he had to do this in a way that wouldn't put his own job at risk. (We talk extensively about surviving a new boss in Chapter 6.)

Stephen's speech to the company seemed to go well, but he needed a reality check from one of his allies to be sure his messages about the new leader got through—and that he hadn't inadvertently burned any bridges. One of Stephen's allies gave him exactly what he needed. She told him that what he had said was just as important as what he hadn't said, and that his comments allowed everyone to read between the lines and start to set realistic expectations. And he'd done it skillfully and in a way that wouldn't jeopardize his relationship with the new boss. All in all, Stephen had come out whole.

Tom Gegax, in his book *Winning in the Game of Life*, suggests that the biggest benefit of peer power is the sounding board peers provide. Gegax maintains that peers can reveal answers we already possess but can't really see.[1] Their feedback provides reliable reality testing that either reinforces or cautions against the direction you're taking.

Three Times a Charm

We can't stress enough how colleagues in the right places can keep you from getting blindsided and finding yourself in one of those I-didn't-see-it-coming moments. The correct information can prevent disasters and even reveal new opportunities inside or outside the company. There are all sorts of ways of tapping into the river of facts that's out there. But if you are planning on acting on the knowledge you picked up, we strongly recommend that you always follow the Rule of Three: Only use information you have confirmed through three unrelated sources. Note that we said *unrelated* sources. This is a time when you can't rely exclusively on your band of brothers. You may need to go outside your organization to get the confirmation you require. Of course, your band may be able to tap into their network of contacts to get you the necessary affirmation.

We love the story of Sabina Muldoon, who leveraged the rule of three to launch her own confectionery business. Headquartered in Rochester, New York, Sabina was a senior vice president of Specialty Confections, with responsibilities for marketing and promoting three national chocolate brands. Over the course of more than 10 years, Sabina had grown her career and reputation with the company.

She'd spent a year preparing to roll out a new product for one of the chocolate-bar brands, and was excited about the launch. But while grabbing coffee at a neighborhood Starbucks, Sabina overheard a conversation in line someone behind her was having on his cell phone about drastic cuts in the marketing budget that were going to be taking place at *her* company. As Sabina eavesdropped, the conversation became more specific. Clearly the guy was with one of her competitors, and the brands he was talking about were hers!

Sabina returned to her office knowing two things: first, that she needed to confirm what she'd overheard, and second, that she'd never complain again about people who talk too loudly on their cell phones in public places. Knowing that slashing marketing budgets is rarely a sign of good things to come, Sabina's first call was to a pal in the accounting department, who confirmed, after being promised absolute confidentiality, that projected budgets showed drastic cuts across the board for her brands. Her next call was to the VP of production, an ally from the days when he ran the distribution division. He didn't directly confirm what she'd heard, but did mention that indeed he had engineers working on retooling machines and changing the production schedule. Her third call, to a major vendor in the Midwest, struck gold. He had heard from a good source that the Specialty Confections board was preparing her brands for sale, along with a couple of other divisions. Rumor confirmed! Three times!

The good news. Sabina had always wanted to start her own confections business, and if it was ever going to happen, this was the perfect time. So she set up a meeting with senior management and, instead of asking for a buy-out on her employment contract, she asked for the chance to buy out one of her own brands. Muldoon Confections launched within three months!

WHEN GOOD ALLIES GO BAD

Despite the many benefits, being part of a band of brothers or sisters is not without risk. And one the biggest risks is that you may find yourself fiercely competing head-to-head with your strongest allies, vying for the same recognition, reward, or promotion. This is an I-didn't-see-it-coming moment waiting to happen. One way to evaluate whether you're likely to find yourself in this kind of situation is to determine whether the culture of your organization is collaborative or competitive.

In a competitive culture, there is always a winner and a loser, and, as a result, everyone is trying to be the brightest shining star. In a collaborative culture, there's less focus on individual achievement because the goal is to achieve success for the organization as a whole. An easy way to differentiate between the two cultures is to consider compensation plans. In collaborative cultures, bonuses are often based on a combination of individual results *and* team/divisional results. In competitive cultures team results rarely count; it's all about individual results. In essence, an organization can function either like a track team, where an individual athlete, such as the sprinter, gets the gold medal, or like a well-coached basketball team, where everyone works together to achieve a team win.

If you are going for the gold in a competitive culture, survival is about charging ahead as an individual, no holds barred. Collaborate environments, on the other hand, are defined by a culture where everyone works well together for the team win, and survival is not just about outward individual competition. Competitive or collaborative, you have to navigate through the ego-system of your organization and find a way to reach the top in sync with and competing with colleagues.

You'd think that figuring out whether your organization

The Corporate Ego-System

Competition is in our genes. Members of all *ecosystems* are always in fierce competition for survival. In the corporation, however, we see this as more of an *ego-system*, since competition to be the best is inherent in everyone, from the playground to the boardroom. Believe it or not, it springs from biologically inborn motives that put us in conflict with one another, according to Steven Pinker, author of *How the Mind Works*. Pinker suggests that since our brains were shaped by natural selection, which is really a competition among genes to be represented in the next generation, there's not enough room on the planet for every organism alive in one generation to have descendants several generations down the road. Therefore, those organisms that successfully reproduce do so to some extent at the expense of other organisms.*

*Steven Pinker, *How the Mind Works* (New York: W.W. Norton & Company, 1997), 48–58.

---

is competitive or collaborative would be an easy thing to do. But it's rarely that simple, because an organization's culture reflects the behavior and expectations of leaders of individual departments and divisions, not just the leadership of the total organization. In other words, there can be competitive divisions in a collaborative company or collaborative divisions in a competitive company. So pay close attention to your immediate supervisor. She's the one who sets the tone.

Gaining Access

In the ego-system of corporations, peer battles frequently break out over scarce resources—the scarcest being *access*. Access is extremely valuable, and almost never given freely. Access puts you in the right power circle and gives you the opportunity to strut your stuff. Access also provides you with insider information that is valuable simply because information is power.

As a rule, you have to be a pretty savvy operator to gain access, and when the stakes get really high, people sometimes do extraordinary things to attain it. We've seen junior managers change their daily train commute in order to end up in the bar car with a division head from their company. We know executives who have gone out of their way to befriend (okay, bribe) the maitre d' at a restaurant frequented by company management to always make a table available for them in close proximity to a senior manager. And get this: At one point in CBS history, *four* senior television executives all moved to the same small New York City suburb in order to be in the same hometown as the president of the network.

At one of the largest financial institutions in New York

City, the CEO announced that the head of the investment bank would be retiring within the year. Everyone inside the company, and several executive search firms in the banking industry, knew there were two key contenders for the position: John Rodgers and Greg Densmore. Each was a president of a major, successful division within the company, and each was well qualified to take over the bank.

John Rodgers was the more senior of the two. Known on Wall Street as one of the "Masters of the Universe," John had a longtime professional relationship with the CEO, was a major producer for the firm, and was exceptionally well respected in the industry. Greg Densmore, his rival, was less seasoned, also a major producer, well liked, charismatic, and very ambitious. Greg wanted to head the investment bank, but he knew that John was the heir apparent. As Greg was plotting how to position himself to compete for the job, he was suddenly transferred to London to head the company's European operations. The transfer made it look like he was out of the running, and his peers saw this as a move by the CEO to send Greg out to pasture and clear the way for John. Greg didn't see it that way. Instead, he devised a one-year strategic plan to ensure his visibility, build a network of new clients, prove his value, and most importantly, take steps that would assure access to senior management.

Greg's first move was to hire a public relations firm, at his own expense, to make sure that his name remained prominent in financial circles on both sides of the Atlantic. Before leaving New York, he used his checkbook and his connections to take on the role of chair for a major New York charity, which would require his presence in New York on a fairly regular basis. When he arrived in London, Greg had his PR firm issue a press release touting his new London assignment and responsibilities. He sent an internal memo to all employees of the bank outlining how he envisioned his new role and explaining how critical Europe was to the company's future growth. Greg also sent impressive, well-timed, clever gifts to the CEO for all special occasions. Over the course of nine months, Greg was exceptionally successful in London and, at the same time, significantly increased his face time with the CEO every time he traveled to New York. At year's end, Greg was brought back from London and named head of the investment bank. His campaign of access and visibility worked.

Greg Densmore understood the critical importance of *access* as should every manager. He maneuvered through the competitive ego-system with style and grace. He displayed mastery at managing relationships and at knowing what was ultimately important for winning the position he wanted. And best of all, he managed to outwit a competitive colleague.

It is important to understand: To get access you do *not* need to have deep pockets or go to extremes like Greg Densmore. But you can still learn an important lesson from his story: You may have to do something unusual to achieve your goals. We once knew a guy who was truly an empty suit—charming but barely competent—a guy who seemed destined to stay a low-level manager his whole life. But he was ambitious. He found out where his boss got his regular haircut and made sure to have an appointment at the same time. Long story short, he eventually became a vice president of the company.

You can use Greg's strategy and persistence in many competitive situations with colleagues. Here's what we suggest:

- If you're thrown a curve on the way to a promotion or new title, don't let it derail or deter you. Take a breath.
- Always plot a visibility strategy. Craft a way to stay on the hiring or promoting manager's radar screen.
- Overachieve and *exceed* your performance goals, and insure that everyone knows you did.
- If you can't create your own groundswell, ask someone you know in the public relations or publicity field to help you.
- Leverage every opportunity and take risks that may allow you to receive more recognition for your accomplishments.

While some of these approaches to gaining access may sound a little extreme, remember this: You are always competing with other people, and you never know what lengths they are willing to go to in order edge you out of the way. So the challenge to you is to ask yourself what you can possibly do to get close to the powers that be and promote yourself. It's all about getting yourself into your boss's comfort zone, and it comes down to this: Either get savvy or get blindsided.

One final note about access: Be very, very careful about getting access to someone who's above your boss. People are often insecure, and something as innocuous as a water cooler chat with the president of your company could be perceived as going over your boss's head or, worse, trying to sabotage her. The best way to handle these situations is to defuse the misconceptions before they happen. For example, you might send your boss an e-mail saying, "The Big Guy just asked to see me. I'll let you know what he says." And then, of course, report back as much and as soon as you can.

Seeking Visibility, Taking Risks

There are ways of increasing your visibility and, therefore, your access, in a competitive environment that may require taking significant risks or even changing the direction of your career. It's worth the gamble if you have confidence in your abilities, are looking for a chance to improve your skill sets, want to find a way to set yourself apart from your peers, and want to broaden your visibility in the company. Be sure to have a strong exit strategy in place before you make the leap.

At CBS, Nancy Widmann was clever enough to roll the dice and leverage an opportunity. She had to decide if an offer presented by the office of the chairman would catapult her career to a higher level in the organization, or stall her climb up the ladder.

Nancy had been with CBS for five years and was the sales manager of the Radio Division when someone from the chairman's office asked whether she would consider a move to a corporate staff position—vice president of placement and recruitment for CBS Inc. Nancy had to weigh the decision very carefully. Her career was moving along nicely. She had, up to this point, held various radio sales jobs and loved that side of the business. She was concerned that moving to HR would mean leaving sales and the broadcasting part of the company. She was also worried that her colleagues would move ahead of her in the promotion derby. Human resources was unfamiliar turf and Nancy was nervous about whether she had the skills required to do a good job. On the other hand, the new position carried a VP title and would add significantly to her knowledge base. More important, it would dramatically increase her visibility at CBS. Nancy decided to roll the dice and took the job.

It didn't take long for Nancy to realize that she'd made the right decision. With her new title, she was immediately able to increase her access to senior management. As vice president of placement and recruitment, she helped devise a diversity-training program for each operating division of the company. And she worked on a recruitment program on college campuses. While working on these programs, she was able to forge a direct line to each division president.

Over the next six months, Nancy was invited to attend senior-level company events, conferences, and staff meetings. Her visibility was increasing every day, but she always kept her lines of communication open with the management of her former division. Nancy saw her former colleagues on a regular basis and attended radio functions whenever possible. After two years in HR, Nancy was appointed senior vice president of CBS radio sales. Eight years later, she became president of the radio division. The risk paid off, in part because she had recognized that the gamble of moving from a line to a staff job was offset by the greater opportunity for visibility and access to senior management.

In Nancy's case, taking a big chance significantly changed the direction of her career and put her on the fast track. But risk taking isn't for everyone. Here's how you can decide whether that gamble you're considering is worth taking:

- You can accept that the risk *might not* pull you ahead of your peers.
- You're ready to leave if things don't work out.
- You have your exit strategy in place and it is current and operative.
- You're going to learn something new that will increase your marketability.
- You'll gain more access to senior management.

Getting a Seat at the Table

Sometimes gaining access can be as simple as knowing where to sit. Real players are masters at choosing the seat that guarantees the most exposure and ensures continued access—in the boardroom, at a staff meeting, at a conference.

Seating politics flow from where the boss takes his place at the table. He is the fulcrum. The true power seat is to the boss's immediate right. The second best seat is to the boss's immediate left. The third power seat, and the one that is usually overlooked, is directly across the table from the boss, in his direct line of sight. So if you're up against a couple of linebackers who won't let you near the top two seats, calmly take number three. But if you do, know that you're going to be called on and make sure you come into the room ready with all the answers.

IT'S NOT ALWAYS FAIR PLAY

Most of the time it's a fair fight. Most of the time talent gets rewarded. Most of the time the good guys—or at least the ones with the best connections—win. But sometimes, more often than we'd like, a colleague-turned-competitor who feels she's losing the battle for access or visibility can become a hazard to your career health.

Insecure peers are often more adept than other colleagues at taking shots or spreading seeds of doubt about your competency. And their weapon of choice may well be *feint praise.* Yes, we know that the expression is "damned with faint praise," with an "a" in *faint.* But in this case the motives of the person doing the praising are more sinister; they're designed to be a fake-out, to give the one doing the praising an opportunity to knock you out of the way. Hence *feint*, meaning "a movement made in order to deceive an adversary; an attack aimed at one place or point merely as a distraction from the real place or point of attack."[2]

Insecure peers have an uncanny ability to drop a little feint praise at just the perfect time in the perfect ear—your boss's. Colleagues of ours often joke about how they like the entertainment business because people don't stab you in the back; they stab you in the front. Well, feint praise is definitely a stab in the back. It's a subtle way of putting peers down without *seeming* to put them down. Feint praise plants the seeds of doubt in the mind of whoever hears it.

Feint praise is pretty easy to recognize. If you hear one of these lines said about you, you've got a big problem on your hands:

- She means well.
- He has too much on his plate.

- With everything she has going on, it's amazing she gets through the day.
- He is under enormous stress.
- In spite of all that, she is such a nice person.
- He is too smart for his own good.
- Doesn't she seem different lately?
- He is so distracted these days.
- She's doing a fantastic job, considering . . .

How do you handle feint praise? First, do not dismiss it. Phrases like the ones just given are not said accidentally. They are a deliberate attempt to blindside you and they have transformed the speaker from simple adversary to full-scale enemy. When dealing with this enemy you have two options:

1. You can quietly have an off-the-record conversation and draw your line in the sand with a clear "back off" message. You might say, "I'm onto you! From now on, don't even think about offering commentary about me."
2. You can freeze the enemy out and isolate her from any important connection to your business at hand.

What you *cannot* do is report the incident to senior management or get caught up playing the same game.

We'd all like to believe that the people we work with are colleagues, working toward the same goals and looking out for each other's interests. Don't fool yourself. If you haven't done so already, you'd better dust off your inner cynic. Yes, there are people you can trust. And when you find them, stick with them—they can help you achieve things in your career that you never would have been able to do on your own. We all have colleagues who worked with us who are still in our lives, still giving guidance, and still rooting for us in every way. But understand that the world of business is highly competitive and sometimes competition brings out the worst in people. So be careful. Doing so will enable you to better evaluate your colleagues' intentions and motives. In our view, it's better to be a little cynical than completely blindsided.

Chapter 4 Takeaways

1. Form your own coalition or band of brothers or sisters.
2. Enter into personal trade agreements with trusted peers.
3. Find a colleague to give you honest reality checks.
4. Remember the Rule of Three. Confirm all hearsay with three *unrelated* contacts.
5. Assess whether your work culture is competitive or collaborative.
6. Take a career gamble if it gives you visibility and access—and if you're ready to walk if it doesn't work out.
7. Confront feint praise by drawing your line in the sand.

5

THE TROUBLE WITH TEAMS

In 1886, German philosopher Friedrich Nietzsche cautioned, "Madness is the exception in individuals but the rule in groups."[1] A couple of generations later, Winston Churchill went one step further: "A committee is the organized result of a group of the incompetent who have been anointed by the uninformed to accomplish the unnecessary."[2]

Anyone who's ever worked on a team knows exactly what Nietzsche and Churchill, who ordinarily don't belong in the same sentence, were talking about: You can get bogged down by the frustration, the agendas, the backstabbing, the power fights, and lazy or manipulative team members. It doesn't matter whether the teams are autonomous, virtual, multitiered, or cross-functional, the story is the same. Companies don't want to make noise about one employee's contribution and impact over another's for fear of damaging morale or creating a star system.

Companies aren't likely to do away with the team system anytime soon. So what can you do? Your goal should be to discover how to *get credit* for good work without coming off like a self-promoter. In team-based cultures, highlighting your successes requires a delicate balancing act.

There are real risks to disappearing inside a team. For the most part, teams foster anonymity and frustrate individuality. Your contributions too easily get buried within the team product, and that's where you can run into trouble. It is easier for team members to slack off when working on a team than when working alone because *accountability* is not directly attributed to each person. It instead gets *dispersed* across the whole team. Author Stephen P. Robbins (*The Truth about Managing People . . . and Nothing but the Truth*) claims this "dispersion of responsibility" leads individuals to expend less effort when working collectively than when working individually. He calls this "social loafing," and believes that teams create a kind of "negative synergy."[3] In other words, many teams are often *less* efficient because individual team members mistakenly think their contribution can't be measured.

If there's any way to avoid working on teams, we say do it. But—and this is a huge "but"—in today's business world, that may not be possible or even desirable. You will most likely get put on a team or appointed to head one, and there may be no graceful way out. Many organizations claim to value teamwork over individual achievement and actually penalize those who don't appear to be team players. Does that mean you have to subjugate your own needs to those of the all-powerful group and risk being lost in the crowd or even blindsided? Not at all.

Years ago, a high-wire act called the Flying Wallendas

edged across the tightrope, team members piled in a pyramid: four at the base, then three, then two, and finally one on the very top balanced so perfectly.

The safety of the *entire team* hinged on each individual's sense of equilibrium; the survival of *each team member* depended on the team functioning as one single unit. There's a lesson here.

One of the challenges of succeeding in business is finding the right balance between looking out for yourself and doing what's best for your business unit. Effective teamwork calls for team effort, but at many organizations, the *real effort* is in making the team *work* while simultaneously securing your own success. And that's not always easy to do. If you overemphasize your identity as a team member, you may not get the credit you deserve. If you push your own agenda and undervalue or ignore the team, you may alienate colleagues, sabotage valuable projects, and get branded as a lone ranger, a loose cannon, not a team player.

Failing to project willingness and an ability to become a contributing member of the team could bring your career to a grinding halt. So how do you keep your balance on the high wire, holding up all those corporate Wallendas on one hand, and maintaining your edge as a hard-driving, talented, and ambitious individual on the other? It won't be easy, but it can be done—if you stick to the following three steps:

1. Analyze your team.
2. Manage your image.
3. Think like an owner.

Let's take a closer look at these three processes.

ANALYZE YOUR TEAM

If you want to compete and win within the team dynamic, you have to do a detailed analysis of the players, the power source, and the goals. No two teams are the same, and the more you know about the one you're on, the better your balancing act will be and the less likely you'll be tripped up. Here are five steps to help you do it.

1. *Do a power survey.* Who's the leader of the team? Where does it get its direction? In most cases the leader of this team will be the boss, but in some cases there is a stronger team member who directs the mandate or activity. Sometimes there's no clear leader at all, and the role can become yours by default. We discuss this later in the chapter.
2. *Identify the team's agenda.* What's on the table, what are the team's primary objectives? What's under the table, the team's secondary or hidden objectives?
3. *Watch for alliances.* With whom are your fellow team members allied? Where do they get their power from? What sorts of relationships—business or personal—between team members could affect the team?
4. *Be a talent scout.* What talents does each of the team members have? What are their strengths and weaknesses? Who are the winners and the losers?
5. *Conduct a personal gap analysis.* What talents do you bring to the team that others don't have? These are the skills you'll want to emphasize the most as projects get assigned.

Keep this checklist handy. You'll need to pull it out every time you join a new team, regardless of its size, mission, or level within your company. Once you've done your due diligence analysis, you're ready to move on to your next challenge: differentiating yourself from everyone else on the team.

MANAGE YOUR IMAGE

If being on a team is unavoidable, it's essential that you always come across as the very model of a team player. Never break cover. This will position you perfectly to support your team and pursue your own goals at the same time. This is tricky. Follow our advice and you'll get better and better at this. And while you're taking the field with the rest of the team, always keep your eye out for opportunities to show your stuff. Earn your teammates' respect by taking on some critically effective roles:

- *Be the solid, go-to guy.* One of the most critical roles is that of the center of gravity—the team member who can be counted on at all times to provide a balanced perspective and get it done when all around you is chaos. This role is often underrecognized but it is essential to the success of the team.
- *Be the cheerleader.* Throw out strategic ideas and make your enthusiastic presence known. Being a cheerleader—providing positive support for the team's ideas—may sound like a lightweight role, but it doesn't have to be. You can be most effective when the team is facing long odds by grasping the situation and providing support to encourage everyone to keep moving toward the team's goals.

- *Bolster the skills of the weakest link.* Offer to cover a meeting, write a report, critique a presentation. Each team member has an equally important role to play, but not everyone can be a superstar in all areas. Ideally, each member's strengths will complement those of the other members. So if someone on the team has weaker skills than you in certain areas, lend a hand. He or she will hopefully return the favor sometime.

- *Always give others credit.* If it's a team effort, it's a team win. Remember not to be too self-serving. Sometimes the important thing is to be a member of the *winning* team and to be recognized for being associated with the movers and shakers in the company.

- *Take risks for the team.* Don't flinch under pressure. When the team makes a decision to take a risk, you, as an individual, have to be willing to take the risk and live with the consequences. No one believes someone who, in the face of failure, tries to dissociate himself from the failure by saying, "It wasn't my idea." Take the good with the bad and you'll be admired as a team player.

THINK LIKE AN OWNER

Team effort doesn't end with managing your image. You have to do more than create a cooperative picture. Winning on a team is about adopting an *ownership mind-set*, thinking and acting as if you have a *personal stake in the outcome* of every project. Owners think differently from non-owners in that they take direct responsibility for the process and the end result. Owners are invested every step of the way. They transcend functional boundaries and, where needed, break, bend, or stretch the rules, as long as doing so better achieves the organization's purpose. Although it can be tough to do in a strong team setting, adopting an owner's mind-set is the best way to achieve success for you and your team. Here's how to think like an owner:

1. *Work with an entrepreneurial focus.* Think, "What would I do if I owned this company?" The most impressive owners are fully identified with the success of their company and are willing to do whatever it takes to achieve the win. They don't worry about the risks; they always focus on what it takes to move the needle.

2. *Create value in your specific discipline to impact the bottom line.* Remember that it's *always* about the money. To be successful your team must either bring in revenue or add value, or support those who bring in revenue or value. If you always have this thought top of mind, you should find a way to remind your team that its primary focus must be to contribute to the bottom line.

3. *Never say, "It's not my job!"* If you're stuck on boundaries, you lose. When this is your perspective, your pure job description becomes irrelevant. If success requires that you answer the phones or spend half a day filing, just jump in and do it. What we're suggesting is that you see the mission, and you get it done. Owners always do!

Okay, so you know how to figure out what's happening on your team, and you've learned some smart ways to manage your image. You even have a mandate to think like an owner. Now let's take a look at the three basic types of teams you may land on, and how to keep your head above water.

THE CORPORATE LEAGUE

Having spent decades in corporate America, we think there are three basic types of teams, each with its own unique configuration and signature, each with its own possibilities for being blindsided. Collectively, these three teams make up the corporate big league. No matter what industry you're in, what kind of organization, or how high up you are in the corporate food chain, at some point in your career you'll have a brush with all three types. But in all cases, your challenge will be how to contribute to team success while assuring your visibility. Let's look at the following types of teams and devise a game plan. The three teams in the corporate league are:

- The dream team.
- The echo chamber.
- The dysfunction junction.

The Dream Team

On the surface, the dream team seems like the perfect environment. It functions like a well-oiled machine. Interactions and relationships between team members are warm and open; everyone's opinions are considered; ideas are shared, consequences weighed, and good products or services created. This is the team bringing in the big bucks.

But curb your enthusiasm. As good as it sounds, the dream team may not be as profitable, functional, or desirous as it might seem on the surface. Dream teams can become nightmares. Consider this story about an international fashion magazine.

The envy of the publishing industry, this extraordinary sales team was led by an experienced and talented publisher. Most of the team members had worked together for more than 10 years and enjoyed a friendly, fun chemistry that extended into their social life. They shared personal trainers and hairdressers. Two had the same interior designer. One team member had a relative who catered top-flight social parties and made sure her colleagues were always on the invite list. When the team beat its numbers month after month, the publisher would invite her staff for weekends at her beach house. Each spring, they all traveled together to the Paris collections. Circulation was at a three-year high, and no one on the team thought the ride would end.

But as the economy cooled, page count, driven by advertising, started to fall off and circulation dropped. The team, still in perfect synch and harmony, bolstered each other at staff meetings, congratulating each other on a great effort, even if the effort did not produce results. No one ever complained about bad performance or bad results because it might have dampened the team's enthusiasm and, anyway, things would improve when the economy picked up.

But things didn't improve. So the team offered excuses for its poor performance and promised senior management that the numbers would get better. Because of their successful track record and complacency, they never noticed that other fashion books were moving in on their territory and stealing their market share. And they never noticed that despite the troubled economy, the other magazines were managing to *increase* ad pages. When the truth finally hit them, they dismissed it, saying that the other magazines were "giving it away" or "that was business not worth having anyway."

With sagging numbers and no tough turnaround initiatives, the CEO, finally out of patience, fired the publisher and brought in a new one. When the team eventually woke up from their dream, they were unemployed. And not a single one of them ever saw it coming.

One of the most significant contributors to team failure can be a long, steady string of wins. It should be a red flag for you. Without anything to shake up behavior, it is too easy for a dream team to become complacent, self-congratulatory, and lazy. When team members are focused inward on making each other feel good, rather than outward on the competition, the likelihood of failure increases—yours and the team's. Here's why being on a dream team can hurt your career.

- You rarely get an accurate assessment of your talents or skills.
- You do not learn new tactics because everyone believes the old ones still work well.
- You lose your competitive edge and perspective about your competition.
- If the team fails, you fail. There is no protection. There are no carve-outs!

If you're on a dream team, there is actually good news and bad news. The good news is that for a period of time you're in the limelight, and that will give you some high visibility. The bad news is that the spotlight will eventually burn out. When that happens, you run the risk of being pushed out along with the entire team. So take advantage of the attention and accolades while you've got it to promote yourself to senior management and use it as a springboard for your career. Keep in mind that good fortune doesn't last forever, and make your jump before it runs out.

The Echo Chamber

Under the pressure of heavier workloads, time crunches, and the constant demand for ever-increasing profits, many companies create teams that become what author Irving L. Janis calls *groupthink* teams.[4] Janis describes groupthink as the "psychological drive for consensus at any cost that suppresses disagreement and prevents the appraisal of alternatives in cohesive decision-making groups." In other words, it's an echo chamber.

The team leader comes up with an idea and the Yeses reverberate through the team: "*YES, yes*, yes, yes, yes." Everyone feeds back to the group leader *exactly* what she wants to hear, and never is heard a discouraging word. This team's conformity forbids anyone, ever, to utter an opinion counter to the leader's view. No one can be pessimistic, disparaging, or negative. Team members wield little or no power individually. There is never a candid or open discussion about issues.

Echo chamber thinking often leads to defective decision making. The team's decisions reflect compromises everyone can live with instead of what's best for the company. The echo chamber team can hurt your career by squashing your individuality, suppressing your creative thinking, and worse, making you a victim when and if the group makes the inevitable bad business decisions.

Early in her career, Nancy Widmann learned first-hand the dangers of groupthink. Jim Hardy, head of the FM stations group at CBS Radio, put together a team of CBS program directors, sales managers, and outside consultants to work on changing the format and call letters for the FM station in San Francisco. As head of the national sales rep firm, Nancy was asked to join the team. The project was expensive, highly researched, and involved deciding on the music for the station, selecting on-air talent, testing themes for the advertising campaign, and the all-important task of choosing the station's new call letters. Everyone knew, from a marketing standpoint, that it was a good idea to pick call letters that would closely sound like the kind of music the station would play.

The research revealed a hole in the market and projected likely success for an oldies station. Jim Hardy was anxious to get the station on the air and to begin programming by the time the fall rating book arrived. The team was presented with a preliminary list of available call letters, and Jim immediately jumped on the call letters "KODS." He saw KODS, Oldies105, as a perfect combination of call letters and format, and wanted everyone on the team to see it that same way. Typically, before confirming call letters, research teams would conduct focus groups to test audience reaction to the letters chosen and to pick up any negative indicators. But Jim didn't want to wait for the focus group results; impatient to launch the station, he convinced the entire team to sign off on the KODS call letters. He left absolutely no room for disagreement or challenge.

Sucked in by Jim's fervor, Nancy was reluctant to voice her disagreement and concern over the call letters choice.

To her ear, KODS, when spoken, sounded like "odious" which means distasteful and offensive, and she sensed these letters would present a competitive problem. Still, Jim's pressure and the group's attitude made her feel she could say nothing. Groupthink prevailed.

It wasn't long before the debacle hit. After spending a great deal of money launching the station, CBS Radio rivals grabbed onto the word *odious* and day after day played with the call letters to their competitive advantage. CBS was not only made fun of publicly, but its expensive marketing campaign bit the dust. The company blew a ton of money because groupthink stifled any challenge at the table. When groupthink suffocates the truth, heads roll. The outside consultants lost their contract and the research director was fired. Jim assigned blame to the team, and Nancy decided it might be time to look around for another position in the company.

We don't think there is much good news associated with being on an echo chamber team *unless* the team leader is a charismatic, larger-than-life, attention-getting player inside the organization. Why? You might be able to make it work to your advantage. If your goal is to get promoted—and whose isn't?—a seat on this team could look like one of the best seats in the house. When the team leader is a superstar and his profile is always rising, people on his team have a shot at shining in reflected glory. Unlike the dream team, the spotlight is solely on the leader, not on anyone around the table. If he succeeds, you go along for the heady ride. We've seen dozens of executives with marginal talent move all the way to the top, dislodging worthy colleagues along the way, because they were members of an entourage, tethered to the right leader. Similar to the dream team, however, you can get blindsided on this team. Often when the charismatic leader falls from his throne, he takes his whole crew down with him.

The Dysfunction Junction

When a team leader loses direction, controls too tightly, abdicates responsibilities, or can't demonstrate clear and achievable goals, the team becomes dysfunctional. And it's all too easy to get caught right in the middle. Not surprisingly, there's not much of a waiting list for membership on this team. But don't be in such a hurry to walk away. The leadership vacuum that is the most prominent feature of a dysfunctional team may present an unexpected opportunity. It did for Lisa Berkowitz, who successfully took over a dysfunctional team at a fast-growing, global bookseller based in Miami.

Lisa signed on as VP of business development, not knowing that her predecessor had quit because she felt she was being smothered by the company's CFO, Joe Rivera, Lisa's new boss. Rivera was dictatorial and insisted that all his direct reports work as a tight-knit team. One of his requirements was a daily update report that he demanded each manager deliver out loud in a sort of dramatic reading at the team meeting. Lisa noted that the managers never discussed problems at these meetings, never shared information with each other, and never objected to Rivera's proposals. What's more, they were intimidated and never offered new initiatives. Worried that her growth in the new job could be severely limited, Lisa decided she could either quit or do something to change the situation.

Since she liked the money, loved living in Miami, and was looking forward to the excitement of a new job, Lisa opted to go for the challenge of reforming this dysfunctional team. She spent a lot of time closely studying Rivera's management style and even more time observing what made the other team members tick. She began to figure out what would satisfy each teammate's needs. Lisa then used her position in business development to integrate her teammates' ideas into her projects and gave them full credit for their plans. Slowly everyone began to share more information with her, which helped her create and present some imaginative new proposals for the company.

She never openly criticized Joe. On the contrary, she was very careful to defer to him in meetings. But she gradually asked a lot of questions that ultimately led to changes in the daily meetings, and the team began to participate in more open exchanges. To get a reality check (see Chapter 4), she asked another VP to evaluate how Rivera was receiving her suggestions. All appeared positive. Because Lisa had the support of the others, and always kept Rivera in the loop, even allowing him to take some credit, he was willing to support her ideas. He became even more supportive when he learned that the CEO loved her proposals. Lisa, in essence, became the de facto leader of the team. Two years later, she received the recognition she deserved and was given Rivera's job.

Lisa recognized that in the abyss of dysfunction, strident tactics wouldn't do the trick because team members were already living with tension and confusion. She was able to leverage the chaos around her with a campaign of quiet persuasion. After first analyzing everyone on the team and their motivations, she continued to salute the leader, even while she was siphoning away his power and taking control. Her plans worked. She knew how to seize the opportunity, take charge, think like an owner, and make a real difference to the bottom line of her organization. Had it not worked, Lisa would have dusted off her exit strategy and headed for the door.

A team with a leader who is nowhere to be found offers another great opportunity for you to shine. During the 25 years he had been with Quartermaine Licensing in San Diego, Richard Lockhardt, executive VP of licensing, had earned an impressive industry-wide reputation. He was considered a guru, having trained countless young account executives on the West Coast who eventually held powerful positions in licensing at Sony and Warner Bros. Revenue was strong. Life was good. So good, in fact, that Lockhardt was approached by an executive search firm to consider an opportunity in Seattle, one where he would lead a new corporation formed from the merger of two young licensing companies. The venture capital firm honchoing the merger wanted a seasoned, experienced executive to take the CEO slot. They made Lockhardt an offer he couldn't refuse. He took the job and moved to Seattle with a firm two-year, no-cut contract in hand.

Lockhardt assembled his team, many from within the merged companies, others from outside. And he brought along from San Diego one of his trusted lieutenants, Gary Tobler. Everyone settled in and the teams from both companies slowly began to work together. But there was a problem. Back in San Diego, business had been so good for so long and his team so experienced that Lockhardt hadn't worked too terribly hard for quite some time. Figuring he could do the same thing in the new job, he stopped showing up for morning strategy meetings, checking in with Gary for updates instead. That kind of hands-off management may have worked in San Diego, but with the new company it was a disaster.

Without a strong leader to meld the two divergent corporate cultures, each faction held onto its old turf and alliances. There was no leader, no forward vision, no guidance, no control, and no sense of mutual interest. It didn't take long for the team members to realize that Lockhardt wasn't in charge, and the company quickly became dysfunctional.

Gary saw the leadership void as an opportunity to pick up the mantle. He grabbed the conch. Loyalty wasn't an issue since Lockhardt was doing nothing more than calling it in and he was damaging the business. Gary recommended to the money people that Lockhardt be bought out and that he would be the right person to lead the operation. Vacuum filled—Gary wins, Lockhardt out.

Both Lisa and Gary made moves because they recognized a clear leadership vacuum and they had risk-taking spirits. If you're on a dysfunctional team and don't have the chutzpah and experience to take the reins, you only have two choices: You'll have to either wait out your ineffective boss and see if another leader emerges from the team or try to find another place in the company.

Whether it's a dream team, an echo chamber, or a dysfunctional team, our suggestions on surviving and determining an action plan will give you time to update your exit strategy. If part of that strategy is to find a new place on the field or join a new team, you can maneuver under cover.

We are close to an executive who was flirting with disaster in a team situation until she followed the recommendations discussed here and was able to navigate a minefield. Jessica Alexander was heading the marketing team in the Chicago office of a large computer company. She reported to Winnie Sun Lee, executive VP of marketing. Jessica had a reputation for creative thinking and frequently introduced innovative, out-of-the-box concepts. Implementing her ideas always managed to shake a few corporate cobwebs loose.

But Winnie Sun Lee began to take issue with Jessica's lack of conformity and questioned her compatibility with the team. Jessica wisely read the room and saw the red flags of a confrontation ahead. She saw it coming. She began quietly meeting with other team leaders in the company in order to identify places where her creative thinking would be embraced and rewarded. Soon, Jessica accepted another position and let Sun Lee know that she had found a team where her creative contribution would be valued and appreciated. Jessica took a bold but necessary step. She moved strategically and cleverly to enhance her career and still stay with the company. This won't work everywhere. Many companies aren't enlightened and don't allow people the freedom to move from one area to another.

You really don't have to be stuck! Many companies have pockets of possibilities where individual achievement will be rewarded. You have to make the necessary moves to maneuver onto teams where your contribution will be recognized. Some are obvious, whereas others are hovering just below the radar. Find them!

While it's important to be able to interpret the signals that are telling you it's time to move, it's even more important to do so before your star begins to fade. It's a lot easier to make a change while you're seen as successful and as having choices and value. Once you begin to lose your star quality, no matter the reason, you run the risk of being seen as tired goods. This is another critical reason to always keep your exit strategy current, so you can pull the trigger while you are still a hot property.

STRATEGIES FOR PSYCHING OUT THE TEAM DYNAMIC

Ultimately, no matter what team you find yourself assigned to, you'll always need to strike a good balance between visibility and supporting your team. We want to suggest some strategies to keep you at center stage and still a good team player. There's no need to get blindsided by a team dynamic if you:

- *Establish a direct line of communication with a senior manager.* This might be a mentor or former boss. Make sure that you let this person know, with notes and calls, what you are doing and the contributions you are making. This manager becomes an advocate for you in the company. You never know when you'll need her help. If the team you are on goes south or blows up, this person will throw you a safety line.
- *Position your accomplishments carefully and strategically.* Remind your mentor or advocate how your achievements benefit the company and the company's management. Be sure and give positive feedback about other team members.
- *Find a moment when you can step into a leadership role.* This is the most essential factor for surviving the team dynamic. If you have a solid idea or you think the team is heading in the wrong direction, stand up and make your voice heard.

Finally, it just might be that you can move forward on a team, surrounded by talented people who are working to achieve a goal. After all, it's more important to be part of something successful than to be mired down in projects that go nowhere. And whatever you do, don't throw away your shades just yet. You can be sure there will come a time when you'll be back in the spotlight!

CHAPTER 5 Takeaways

1. Get credit for your work but don't come off as a self-promoter.
2. Analyze your team and watch for alliances.
3. Do a personal gap analysis.
4. Always give credit to others and be the "go-to" guy.
5. Think like an owner and work with an entrepreneurial focus.
6. Determine whether you're on a dream team, stuck in groupthink, or in the middle of dysfunction junction.
7. Find an advocate in the company who will sponsor your success.
8. Have the courage to fill the leadership vacuum on a team.

6

SURVIVING A NEW BOSS

It was 5:30 A.M. and Chase Wenders was stuck on the 405 freeway on the way to his office in Century City. The ring of his cell phone startled him, and looking at the caller ID, Chase saw it was Bob Withers, the chairman of his company. "Joe just walked," Withers said. "He's going to Victory Records. Senior staff, my office, 9:00 this morning."

Chase had been with Caprice Records for five years, and had moved quickly through the ranks to executive VP. He reported—at least until that day—to Joe Dardenne, who had been with Caprice for over 10 years. At first, Chase was stunned, and as he drove along, all he could focus on was who would replace Joe. How long would it take for the chairman to give someone the nod? Would he have a shot at the top slot? Would one of his colleagues beat him out? Would Joe's departure jeopardize the deals he had in motion? But as he pulled off the freeway, it dawned on Chase that there had been plenty of signs that Joe was looking outside, signs that he and everyone else in the division had chosen to ignore. Yep, when he really thought about it, Chase knew that he could have seen it coming.

There are a lot of ways to lose a boss, and there are a lot of ways to find out about it. Some retire. Some get promoted. Some get fired. And some, like Chase Wenders' boss, start to secretly meet with competitors on company time and then leave for greener pastures. Sometimes you read about your boss's departure in the *Wall Street Journal*. Sometimes you hear about it through the grapevine. Sometimes the boss announces he's leaving a few months in advance. And sometimes you come in to work and find an unfamiliar face in the corner office.

Since companies or divisions usually reflect the personality of the top dog, losing that person has a profound effect on the entire organization. After all, the old boss had a specific style, performance expectations, and a defined inner and outer circle of people he trusted—a regular routine. Even if you didn't agree with the way he operated, at least you knew your place at the table and you knew what to expect. The old adage, "The devil you know is better than the devil you don't know," certainly holds true in this situation. But when the old devil starts packing his bags, the atmosphere changes, big-time.

Bottom line: A change in the power structure at the top affects everyone in the company. Picture a line of dominoes. If the first one topples, the rest in line fall sequentially. That's exactly what happened at General Electric when Jack Welch retired. Three senior executives, Jeffrey Immelt, Bob Nardelli, and Jim McNerney, were vying for the top job. When Immelt got the nod, the other two left to head Home Depot and 3M, respectively. Moving down a rung, another exec, Larry Johnston, left GE when he didn't get promoted into one of the three newly open jobs. Johnston left to run Albertsons. Call it a corporate twist on geology and meteorology: As the weather changes on the highest peaks, the tectonic plates under the rest of the mountain range start shifting.

However it happens, changes at the top can create unparalleled opportunity *if* you're prepared. In this chapter, we focus on how shifts in power can affect you and your career, how you can leverage those changes to your advantage, and how to avoid being blindsided.

I LOVE THE SMELL OF CHAOS IN THE MORNING

Anthropologists have long observed that, just before a shift in power among tribal leaders, the tribes' rituals and behaviors change. This phenomenon happens in the corporate jungle as well. Picture one of those classic scenes from every *National Geographic* documentary you've ever seen. The animals are peacefully gathered around the watering hole, relaxing after a tough day on the veldt. Suddenly, something almost tangible runs through the crowd. Something's out there. They may not know exactly what it is, but it's there. The animals tense, lift up their noses, sniff the air, and then, without warning, they charge off in a thousand different directions.

Corporate animals respond in much the same way. When change is in the air, behaviors and alliances are no longer predictable. Everyone is anxiously sniffing around, hoping to get a handle on what's happening. It starts with rumor and conjecture and moves quickly to anxiety, turmoil, and at times dysfunction. It's an extremely stressful and dangerous time. And just like with the animals, it's a time when the weak ones get killed, picked off by something they never saw coming.

There are any number of reasons why a boss might lose power. He could be toppled in a coup and forced to leave. She could be squeezed out as the result of a merger or acquisition. Or managers even higher up the ladder might be disgruntled that your boss isn't making her numbers. While you may be unhappy to see your boss leave, right now it's all about you. And as your boss's stock nosedives, the tether that connects you to him could start to drag you down, too.

In most cases, bosses don't just drop off the face of the earth with no warning. There are almost always red flags. When your boss is losing power, you can often read it through shifts in her performance, relationships, and behavior. Indications of the power loss get confirmed by gossip and through subtle behavioral changes from her direct reports and your colleagues.

The bad news is that most people don't recognize the signs until after the fact. But the good news is that if you pay attention, there's a good chance that you'll be able to recognize and interpret them before the axe drops and take the necessary steps to protect your career.

On an individual basis, any one of these following signs should signal to you that your boss's role is changing, but if two, three, or more of them are true, consider yourself warned.

You Know Your Boss Is Losing Power When . . .

- He is rarely available or he is more available.
- She suddenly starts working from home more often.

- His secretary changes her work habits.
- Her boss calls you for information on pending deals.
- His clients are holding up agreements.
- Her calls to HR and the legal department are no longer returned promptly.
- He increases his travel schedule.
- She sets unrealistic goals and objectives for her staff.
- His door is constantly closed.
- He no longer seems to have insider information on reasons for key decisions.

Bruce Romano, vice president of children's fiction at Howard Publishing, was a manager who misread the signs that his boss was losing power. His boss and division head, Tina Jackson, asked Bruce for his input on a new three-year plan she was preparing for top management. In the past, Tina had always listened to her staff's recommendations and made projections that were realistic and achievable. This time, though, although she went through the motions of asking for Bruce's input, none of the information he delivered made it into the final report. In Bruce's view, Tina was off-base in her projections and her long-range financial plan was unattainable.

Bruce couldn't figure out why Tina was presenting unreachable targets. He asked for clarification, but Tina dismissed his challenge as unduly alarmist and made it clear that she expected Bruce to support her strategy, regardless of what he thought.

Here's what Bruce missed. When Tina rejected his recommendations, he should have suspected that something was amiss. Setting unrealistic goals is often an attempt to shore up diminishing support from higher management, and it frequently signals that a manager is losing power. Whether Tina was trying to curry favor with senior management because her position was no longer secure or she just wasn't planning to be around when the numbers were tallied up, it was clear—but not to Bruce—that Tina wasn't fully invested in the numbers. The danger to Bruce was that he could very easily be held responsible for not meeting the goals down the line.

Managing up (which we discuss in Chapter 7) is a real challenge when your boss is losing power. When you face this situation, as did Bruce, you have two options:

1. Hunker down and wait it out. Something is bound to happen.
2. Go for the brass ring and campaign to take over your boss's job.

Each of these options is dependent on circumstances like time in grade and your personal career objectives. Let's examine both in detail.

Hunker Down

Hunkering down is the best choice in situations where you really have no idea who will be left standing after the dust settles. At the very least, it buys you time. So find yourself a nice bunker, and wait for the bullets to stop flying. But there are two very important caveats:

1. *Remember that laying low is a temporary solution.* There is no definitive timetable for a change of leadership, and we've seen plenty of situations where a weakened leader has been able to hold on for quite a

while. For that reason, make sure you don't stay out of sight for too long.

2. *Don't do anything that even remotely looks like you're taking sides.* If you're waiting out the storm, wait quietly. It is a huge mistake to jump into the "pick the new boss" sweepstakes. You don't have enough information to make an informed decision. And you don't have enough political savvy to know which way the cards will fall. This strategy is best suited for managers who are in the earlier stages of their careers or are new to a team or a division. This positioning can be very effective for those who are planning to leave an organization, either to begin a new business or to change careers.

Go for the Brass Ring

This option is more aggressive and not at all for the faint of heart. Your boss's departure has opened up a tremendous opportunity to sell yourself to the powers that be as a manager with strong leadership skills and vision. So if you truly believe you can fill your boss's shoes, go for it!

Keep in mind, though, that there are some risks. For example, you might be seen by others as disloyal. Also, you don't know if senior management has plans in place for replacing your boss and is ready to make an announcement. Worst of all—and this sometimes happens—your boss may regain his power. If that happens it's pretty much guaranteed that he's not going to be happy to find you with your feet up on his desk.

Given the risks, why would anyone consider this option? Simply put, this might be the chance of a lifetime to prove your value, land a promotion, and make a significant contribution to the organization. So if you're ready to rumble, put together a knockout presentation that's objective, analytical, and focused on the best interests of the company. Over the years, we have worked with many successful executives who, at some critical point in their careers, took the risk and grabbed the brass ring. They couldn't have done it without an ambitious spirit and a gambler's heart.

AND THE WINNER IS . . .

Chances are that you aren't really interested in taking over your former boss's job. Even if you are thinking of taking a shot, we should talk about the reality that it will go to someone else.

Once the name is announced, you need to start positioning yourself to succeed under the new regime and to make it safely through the minefield. It doesn't matter whether the new guy is coming from inside or outside your organization. What does matter is whether you're able to leverage this shifting power balance to your advantage. We believe you can, by deploying the following four key strategies:

1. Do your reconnaissance.
2. Nail your audition.
3. Be a native guide.
4. Watch for sacred cows.

Do Your Reconnaissance

The second you find out who's moving into that vacant corner office, it's essential that you find out everything you possibly can about her. Your goal is to develop a complete picture of your new boss. Hit the phones. Use the Internet search engines. If you know someone who might know anything useful about the incoming boss, make the call. Forget about six degrees of separation—we're interested in two degrees! We guarantee that you'll find more sources of valuable information than you ever imagined possible. When doing your recon, you need to focus on two main areas:

1. What is the new boss's history?
2. What is his management style?

The better you're able to answer these questions, the more you'll be protected against being blindsided.

The New Boss's History

Start by putting together a picture of her professional track record. Where did she work and what jobs has she held before taking the job above you? How long did she stay in each of her previous positions? This information could give you some insight into her intentions. Will she stay long enough to build a successful team and be held accountable for performance, or will she appear on the scene, make a bunch of changes, and then move quickly to yet another enticing high-profile opportunity?

As you're running your background check, be sure to investigate her hiring and firing pattern. That will give you a better idea of whether she tends to keep her newly acquired teams together or break them up. And finally, try to identify whether she travels alone or brings her own team with her. Knowing that will help you plan out your audition strategy and give you a heads-up about sacred cows.

Inside, Outside, and Inside-Out

In many cases, your new boss will come from inside the company. If so, he'll already know the business and the organization's culture. He could be someone you know—the guy who sat next to you at the last department staff meeting—or he could come from another division. His new job might be a lateral move, or it could be a promotion. As is true for virtually everyone in every company, executives who get promoted from within tend to maintain existing relationships and networks that stay constant across moves.

However he got there, your new leader comes into the job with a history of corporate political connections. If you're one of those connections from a previous job, you could do well. But if the new boss doesn't know you, or hasn't had any experiences with you in the past, you'll be in the precarious position of needing to prove your worth, set perceptions, and guarantee your performance.

On the other side of the coin, it's getting more and more common for companies to fill vacant positions from the outside. Why? Too often it's because top management gets it into their heads that someone with no history in the company will have the magic touch. This belief is firmly entrenched in many organizations, despite growing evidence that superstars at one company rarely repeat their successes elsewhere. A 2003 study by Booz Allen Hamilton found that 85 percent of companies that brought in outsiders as CEOs produced below-average returns for shareholders, whereas 55 percent of companies that promoted insiders into the top spot produced better-than-average returns.*

The same dismal results happen outside the C-suite. For example, between 1988 and 1996, only 3 out of 24 investment banks that brought in star analysts from outside the company were able to successfully integrate them into their organizations.†

Despite this rather dismal evidence, there's a good chance that at some point in your career you're going to be working for someone brought in from outside the company. This isn't necessarily bad news. In fact, having a complete stranger take over gives you a wonderful, clean-slate opportunity to shine and impress. But the downside is that if the new boss arrives with her own team in tow, you may have to activate your exit strategy.

If the new leader comes from outside the company but inside your industry, consider yourself lucky. He'll likely be knowledgeable and experienced and, best of all, he speaks your language. Assuming you have your game plan ready, he should easily spot your talents and expertise. However—there's always a however—you may be faced with a boss who thinks he already knows everything there is to know about the business in general, and your company specifically. If his previous company was more successful than yours, he's

*Booz Allen Hamilton Consulting, "Corporate Turnover Study" (New York, 2003).
†Boris Groysberg, Ashish Nanda, and Nitin Nohria, "The Risky Business of Hiring Stars," *Harvard Business Review* (May 2004), 92–100.

(Continued)

probably being brought in to shake up the troops and boost the bottom line. Overall, more than any other new boss, one from within your industry comes with preconceived notions about his role, your business, your company's problems—and possibly about you and your staff.

Keep in mind that this new boss has the same ability as you to do reconnaissance, and you can be sure that he has scoped you out. One positive here is that unlike someone who has taken the position from inside your company, he probably has no personal history with you.

If your new boss comes from outside your industry, his first challenge is to learn the business. Your company's senior management must have been attracted by his proven leadership skills and history of success. And they probably believe that a strong executive is a strong executive and doesn't need any industry-specific knowledge to lead.

Finally, be aware that a new leader, from inside or outside the company, may have been brought in to clean house. There is the danger of severe cutbacks and wholesale staff changes, and you have to be very careful not to be caught in the undertow.

The New Boss's Management Style

The second vital piece of recon focuses on identifying the new boss's management style. Unfortunately, you won't be able to do much of this on the Internet. Understanding your boss's management style is critical, however, if you want to effectively respond to and interact with him from the beginning. Talk to people who have worked with or for your new boss to ask about his behavioral quirks and preferences. Ask everyone who might know, "What's he like to work with?" Here are some specific questions to ask:

- Is she decisive or noncommittal?
- Does he delegate or micromanage?
- Is she fair or arbitrary?
- Is he a team player or a dictator?
- Is she confident or is she insecure?
- Is he diplomatic or acerbic?
- Does she enjoy debate or avoid conflict?
- Does he display tolerance or impatience?

Nail Your Audition

When you've done enough reconnaissance to have a well-drawn picture of the new boss, you'll be ready to focus on your initial meeting. A lot of people assume that they have a 60-day grace period when a new boss arrives, but nothing could be further from the truth. Starting on his first day in office, your boss is identifying those who can and cannot help him achieve his goals.

Years of research on "impression formation" in interviews confirms that people decide about a candidate's competence and potential fit in the *first 90 seconds* of an interview.[1] After that, the interviewer is simply looking for data to support her initial take of "Yes, she'll be great here" or "No, he will never work out!"

Your boss's sorting process starts from the first moment he sees you in the corridor. Over the next few months, as the auditions continue, he'll be deciding whom to keep, whom to promote, and whom to toss. Knowing your boss's history and management style increases the likelihood that you'll make the cut and that you'll be able to make that all-important first impression a real zinger.

How do you handle an audition when you know the new boss has done recon on you and has perhaps heard things about your style that give him pause? The answer is that your recon about his history and management style has to be thorough enough to give you the opportunity to change or offset any negative perceptions a new manager may have about you.

Henry Washburn is an example of a young, impatient executive who used the information gleaned about his incoming boss's likes and dislikes as a basis for changing his own style. Henry was an aggressive, demanding, results-oriented executive, and his personal management style was well known throughout the company. Henry's reconnaissance had revealed that his new boss, Jeff Larson, was quite the opposite: a seasoned, professorial, relationship-oriented type of leader who had a reputation for rambling on and never getting to the point in a discussion. What's more, he enjoyed talking with his staff about politics, sports, and food.

Henry realized that their two styles were hardly a match. And he knew that Jeff—who had been doing his own recon on Henry—would see it the same way. But armed with this information, Henry knew the kind of image he'd need to present at his first face-to-face with Jeff, and the preconceived perceptions he'd have to overcome. The stakes were high; if Jeff thought for a moment that he and Henry couldn't work together, Henry's position could be in jeopardy.

So Henry took the smart career move of making some subtle changes designed to portray himself as someone Jeff would be comfortable having on his team. To accomplish this, he simply put aside a long must-do list for the department and focused instead on having a friendly, relaxed conversation. In their first meeting, Henry engaged Jeff in a rollicking discussion of favorite restaurants, baseball standings, and weekend houses. Henry successfully managed his audition, and Jeff ended the meeting convinced he wanted Henry on his team.

Be a Native Guide

Even if your new boss has been a successful executive elsewhere, what worked for him in his old culture may not work in the new one. Herein lies your opportunity. He'll come on board needing team members who can educate, inform, and get him up to speed. No matter how well he's been briefed, he can't possibly be savvy about the company's internal power structure. He'll need a quick primer on how decisions are made, how people interact, and internal politics.

You can provide that insight, serve as a native guide, and help him immediately get with the program. Your new manager may need your advice even more if he's an industry outsider who needs to get up to speed on your products, your competitors, and corporate strategy. Taking on this role buys you extended audition time and certainly increases your visibility. Ideally, this can solidify your relationship and help secure your position on his team.

Acting as the native guide is often a positive move, but it has its perils. To start with, in and of itself, being a native guide does not guarantee a permanent seat at the new table. Some new leaders simply don't absorb native guides into their operations after the initial indoctrination. Others don't want to work with members of the previous guard and prefer to launch their initiatives by building a brand-new team. The second danger in serving as native guide is that of blurred boundaries. When a new leader starts to feel too dependent on his native guide, or the native guide starts to assume a peer relationship with the new leader, the boss-subordinate boundary gets out of balance and your position is at risk.

If you're in this situation, how do you safeguard yourself and avoid getting derailed? Keep your native guide role secondary to performance. Your new boss absolutely must see you as a significant contributor to the bottom line. If you're a company star, there's a much stronger chance that your position will be secure. There is, of course, no official guarantee, which is why it's always a good idea to dust off your exit strategy just in case you bump up against an I-didn't-see-it-coming moment.

Carol Cohen was an executive asked to serve as native guide but smart enough to be wary. Carol had worked for a major television network for 10 years. She had begun her career in program operations and steadily moved her way up the corporate ladder to a position in program development. Two years into the job, Carol was named senior vice president of program development. Her team continued to be successful and innovative.

That fall, the network was bought by another entertainment company, and the management teams of both organizations were merged. Carol was surprised to hear that a senior manager from the acquiring company would be her new boss. He was a legend in the business. Carol was asked by the head of programming to stay in the division and to help the newly named executive VP learn the ropes. She agreed, but was clever enough to know there would be no guarantee that the new leader would keep her in her role.

For three months, Carol played the native guide and offered critical direction on internal politics and talent issues. At the same time, Carol tapped into her band of sisters and discovered that there would soon be a new position opening in the affiliate relations department. When her new boss presented a consolidation plan for the department, cutting costs and staff, and explained to Carol that he was combining jobs and would not have a place for her in his reorganization, Carol was prepared. She officially made her bid for the job in affiliate relations and asked her new boss to support her move. He endorsed Carol's decision and thanked her for seeing him through the transition.

Watch for Sacred Cows

New leaders often bring sacred cows, a senior executive's entourage, who accompany a powerful executive into a new company. They can come on board when the new boss enters the scene, or they can be summoned by him in the early months after the transition. Sacred cows are trusted members of an executive's team, and usually have a long track record of success and share a common history. They have the distinction of being the most loyal, but not necessarily the most talented.

Sacred cows have mastered the rules of the game; they always protect their boss's back and they never outshine the master (lessons we discuss in Chapter 7). They provide a vital service for a new leader because they can be relied on in a climate of fast decision making, quick turnaround, or political turmoil. They provide a sense of security, confidentiality, and familiarity.

We've worked with many a sacred cow and believe us, it's easy to spot them. Here are the six most common breeds.

1. *The gatekeeper.* This is the trusted loyal assistant. She does all the scheduling and monitors all movement in and out of the corner office. Most gatekeepers follow their boss from job to job and take care of the boss's personal appointments as well as professional. Controlling access makes this the most powerful sacred cow.

2. *The enforcer.* This is the critical team member for the executive who hates conflict. He serves as second in command or sergeant-at-arms and tackles difficult administrative issues. He has the authority to cut budgets, slash costs, and do pretty much anything he wants, all in the boss's name. If you ever get fired, he could be the one you'll hear it from.

3. *The numbers guy.* In most cases, this is the CFO. He sets the budgets and interprets the numbers for the boss. He controls expenses. The CFO is always close at hand. After all, the boss never knows when he might get one of those pesky profit questions.

4. *The protégé.* This is a younger version of the boss. The relationship between these two people is that of a mentor and an adoring acolyte. In many organizations, protégés are often given roles that really stretch their abilities, many times jobs that are way over their head.

5. *The first pal.* This sacred cow is often underestimated. Although he may carry a rather unassuming

title, his function for the boss may go beyond what is declared publicly. He is always at the boss's side, dresses in a similar style, and may even commute with the boss daily. His sole function is to protect his boss and keep him company.

6. *The court jester.* This is the person who serves to ease the tension. He is usually a good storyteller. People like him. At just the right moment, he can provide the comic relief. He makes the boss laugh. He looks powerless, but he isn't.

Sacred cows present a risk to you only if you ignore their power or don't know how to recognize and leverage it. They present an opportunity in that they have influence with the boss and can be your advocates. In their book *The 48 Laws of Power*, which delves into power relationships in the courts of early kings, Robert Greene and Joost Elffers paint a picture of sacred cows that rings just as true for most of the ones we've met. "Great courtiers throughout history have mastered the science of manipulating people. They make the king feel more kingly, they make everyone else fear their power. They often end up more powerful than the ruler, for they are wizards in the accumulation of influence."[2]

Peter Glenn found a way to successfully make a sacred cow into his advocate. Working at a manufacturing company in St. Louis, Missouri, Peter suddenly found his job threatened when a new CEO came in and brought his first lieutenant, Mark Sanchez, along for the ride. Mark had worked with the CEO in all of his previous positions at various companies. Almost immediately after the CEO came on board, the company was presented with the opportunity to make a prize acquisition, and the CEO named

Mark to head up the acquisition team. Peter felt he could make a contribution and impress the CEO, if he were on the team, but knew it would never happen unless he could gain Mark's trust.

Peter's goal was to get on the team. Mark's goal was to successfully make the acquisition. Peter knew the acquisition was important to the CEO and the future of the company and that Mark had to deliver the deal. He decided to boldly present his credentials to Mark as someone who had the talent and insider information necessary to help broker the deal. Mark appreciated Peter's candor and ambition and put him on the team. He successfully completed the acquisition and recommended Peter to the CEO for a promotion.

As Peter cleverly realized, a key strategy with sacred cows is to co-opt them. Sacred cows are locked in place and wield a great deal of power. Because of that, work to align with them and make them your advocates, just as did Peter. But one warning: Do not ever go behind the back or try to compete head-to-head with a sacred cow. You won't survive—guaranteed.

WHEN YOUR PEER GETS THE NOD

At least once in your career you'll find yourself in the un-enviable position of watching helplessly as a peer gets promoted over you. If it hasn't happened yet, it will. It might be politics, it might be personalities. Or it might even be based on the need for someone with different skills than you possess. But that's not going to make it feel any better.

When one person is promoted over his peers, the amigo, the compadre, suddenly becomes *el capitán*. The friend becomes the boss. One of "us" is now one of "them." This necessitates restructuring the relationship dynamics that may have been years in the making. On the one hand, shared history makes a peer promotion a boon to the team and the company, because the group quickly starts from a solid foundation of nuanced work dynamics and a history of trust. On the other hand, that same shared history can make colleague promotions challenging for both parties.

It is never wise to rely on a former relationship with a colleague when he or she has been promoted, because the stakes have changed. (Chapter 2, "Taking the Reins," discusses this situation from the opposite angle.) If you want to secure your role in this situation, you'll have to announce your loyalty and commitment to your new leader. Your former peer needs to know that he has people working for him who will support his success. Getting with the program is essential. Your peer was promoted. You were not. Be clear in your efforts to get behind your colleague's promotion. If you're not sincere, a disconnect between your intentions and your behaviors will be very apparent. We all know this is a critical suck-it-up challenge!

For four years, Helen Martin was the highest producing senior account executive for Open Channel Radio in San Diego. Her passionate goal was to be the next sales manager. But when the job opened up, Helen didn't get it. The new sales manager was a former colleague from the Los Angeles office who happened to be one of senior staff's golden boys. Helen was devastated. This was *her* job; she had earned it and everyone expected it would go to her.

Okay, so now what? Helen pulled herself together and took the long walk down to her new boss's office to offer her congratulations. Every salesperson looked up as she walked by. The air was heavy with tension. She sat down, welcomed her new superior, and filled him in on any office politics he might need to know about. More importantly, she offered to help train two rookies on the staff. Calm settled over the office. The new boss assumed control quietly and effectively. Without a doubt, senior management heard about Helen's cooperative style. Six months later, she was rewarded with a promotion to run the sales staff in New York at corporate headquarters, a far more significant job with a faster, more visible track to the top of the company.

Helen turned what could have been a disaster into a success because she understood that the business world is seldom fair and that everyone was watching to see *how* she lost. Anyone can be a graceful winner, but everyone always roots for a classy loser. How you react to losing a promotion is just as important as how you react to winning. Take a deep breath and make sure that your new boss, and everyone else in the company, knows you are choosing to stay on the team and that you'll still give 110 percent.

Successful leaders learn how to leverage change at the top. They don't get blindsided by organizational power shifts, promotion politics, or management missteps. On the contrary, they see these roadblocks as opportunities to maneuver strategically and to develop a mutually advantageous relationship with their new boss. They learn the art of spotting trouble before it hits, and determining the right course of action. If it's best to leave the organization, they know how to put an effective exit strategy in place. If it is best to stay, they learn how to respond to warning signs and plot their success regardless of who moves into the corner office.

CHAPTER 6   Takeaways

1. Power shifts at the top filter down through the company.

2. Losing a boss can be a dangerous time, but also a time of great opportunity.

3. Commit to memory the 10 signs that indicate your boss is losing power.

4. Before the new boss arrives, do your reconnaissance and compile a profile of job history and management style.

5. Remember, your new boss will make a judgment about you in 90 seconds.

6. Be careful before stepping into the role of native guide. Some bosses don't offer guides a permanent seat at the table.

7. Recognize sacred cows and make them your advocates.

8. Smile and jump on board when a peer gets promoted.

7

Managing the Rank above You

There are all sorts of conflicting theories about the best way to run a company or the fastest way to move ahead in your career. But one thing pretty much everyone agrees on is that your boss is by far the most influential person in your work life.

Over the years we've read dozens of business books, many of which use sports metaphors to describe work situations. While we generally don't believe in following trends, we decided to introduce a sports metaphor of our own to describe your relationship with your boss—just not one you'd expect: tetherball.

You probably remember this game from your grade school playground. It's pretty simple. There's a tall metal pole planted firmly in the ground, with a long cord attached at the top. At the other end of the cord a ball is tied. No matter how hard you hit the ball, which direction it's headed, or how fast it's going, the ball remains attached to the pole.

Much the same is true of your relationship with your boss—and we're sure you can guess which one of you is the pole and which one is the ball. For as long as you're in the game, like it or not, you're firmly attached to your boss—to his history, his reputation, his politics, his strategies, and to some extent his career trajectory.

This attachment can be either a blessing or a curse, sometimes offering great opportunities but also some major traps. It can be a peaceful pasture or a dangerous minefield. How closely you entwine yourself with your boss will affect *your* reputation, how others perceive you, and will have a major influence on what you can accomplish on the job and even where your career goes. In short, your relationship with your boss can make the difference between success and failure. Fortunately, you can alter the terms and gain some control of the relationship. But first, you'll need to learn how to deal with your boss's expectations, perceptions, and management style.

Once you learn how to manage your boss—which is exactly what we show you how to do in this chapter—you'll be well positioned to take charge of your career and you'll have a better understanding of your prospects within your company. Best of all, learning how to effectively handle your boss will go a long way toward keeping you secure. We don't want you shaking your head in an unemployment line and muttering to yourself, "I never saw it coming . . ."

THE PLAYBOOK

Let's face it. You're going to have a tough time maneuvering within your company and advancing your career without your boss's support and backing. Through our own experience in the trenches and from coaching dozens of executives, we've identified five laws that you absolutely must follow if you have any expectation of creating, maintaining, and managing a productive relationship with your boss. These are:

1. Never outshine the master.
2. Make your boss look good.
3. Exceed expectations.
4. Bring solutions, not problems.
5. Protect the boss's back.

Never Outshine the Master

If you're trying to get ahead, it pays to be smart, clever, and to maneuver deftly. But if you're outsmarting, outwitting, or outmaneuvering your boss, you're making a serious error. As Robert Greene, author of *The 48 Laws of Power*, puts it, "When it comes to power, outshining the master is perhaps the worst mistake of all."[1]

Managers who forget this lesson pay a steep price. At the quarterly meeting of a large, well-known manufacturing company, senior management and the entire sales force were meeting on Hilton Head Island for a four-day corporate pep rally. Ken Reynolds, the newly named executive VP of sales and operations, had been with the company for more than 10 years, but was getting his first shot at running the sales retreat. At the opening session, Ken bounded onto the stage to cheerfully welcome all 350 members of the team. With his usual humor and gusto, he entertained and dazzled not only the senior members of the company, but also new arrivals to the various sales forces. He then introduced the CEO, who gave a variation of the same dry, soporific speech that he'd given at every meeting for the past decade.

Over the next three days, Ken continued to be the center of attention. He held court, ran the golf tournament, gave out the sports awards, and every evening before dinner, delivered a humorous toast to the assembled crowd. At all sales meetings, client events, and board functions, Ken was the master of ceremonies, and his reputation as the personality of the company continued to grow.

With company sales stronger than ever, Ken was riding high. But completely out of the blue—or at least that's the way it seemed to Ken—the CEO announced a complete reorganization of the company, and moved Ken from sales to strategic planning. The CEO announced Ken's reassignment as a promotion, but the reality was that Ken no longer held any real power—and everyone in the company knew it. Just six months later, he tendered his resignation.

Although Ken maintained that he was surprised by the reorganization, he really should have seen it coming. He had wrongly assumed that his stellar sales performance made him untouchable, but he let his ego supersede his judgment. He was continually outshining the master! As a result, he got sent to corporate Siberia by an insecure leader who saw Ken's likeability and obvious talents as a threat.

Does not outshining the master mean that you have to dumb down your performance? Absolutely not. Always do your best work and sparkle away—just do it in a way that complements your boss's strengths. That way you'll never be perceived as a competitor. To paraphrase Abraham Lincoln, there's no limit to what you can achieve in your company as long as you make sure your boss gets the credit.

Make Your Boss Look Good

The flip side of not outshining the master is to do whatever you can to ensure that your boss looks as good as possible. So instead of trying to get your name up in lights, you should be your boss's biggest fan, finding countless opportunities to applaud and tout his successes. Do this inside and outside the organization, up and down the chain of command, to his bosses, and to your staff.

Now let's be clear here: We're not talking about blindly sucking up. Instead, we are suggesting a smart game of professional flattery. (See sidebar.) Becoming an accomplished flatterer instantly positions you as a manager who not only is ambitious but also supports company objectives. Standing with your boss this way enables you to leverage your relationship with him to your advantage and builds your own power base.

Making your boss look good is a particularly effective strategy for earning the trust of a boss who is something of a control freak and who keeps you on a short tether. That was the advice that we gave to Vickie Bakasumo, an executive at a large international watch manufacturer. Vickie's boss was a retired army colonel whose previous job was CEO of a major packaged foods company, where he had a stellar reputation. Unfortunately, he didn't know the first thing about the watch business. But that didn't stop him from managing the company as if he were still commanding a combat brigade. "Here's the plan—follow it" was his motto.

Right from the start, Vickie saw that while many of the new boss's strategies might have been brilliant for selling salad dressing, they weren't going to work in the watch business. Not wanting to push back too hard or risk making

---

Sucking Up or Flattery?

The difference between sucking up and professional flattery is subtle but very significant and worth spending another minute discussing. And that difference can be summed up in one word: *sincerity*. If what you're saying is true and you're honestly applauding your boss's expertise or accomplishments, it's flattery. It doesn't matter whether it's just you and the boss in an elevator, whether you're giving a speech, running a staff meeting, or even chatting with a coworker on a bathroom break. But if you're making stuff up because you think that's what the boss wants to hear, it's sucking up.

Motivation also plays a role here. When you're sucking up, it's all about you. You're simply trying to promote your own cause by currying favor. But when you're flattering, it's all about the boss. Yes, you're also protecting yourself and boosting your own stock at the same time, but your main objective is to support the boss and make him look like the star of the show.

---

her boss look foolish, she'd initially agreed that she was on board with the CEO, and then began to slowly suggest alternatives she knew would be more effective. She was very careful to do this in a way that didn't come across as too aggressive. She always backed up her suggestions with well-reasoned and thorough explanations.

Initially, Vickie's boss dismissed her ideas out of hand. But over time, he came to see that she knew what she was talking about. More importantly, he saw that Vickie's alternative approaches were achieving the goals he'd set and were driving growth. The board of directors was thrilled. As his confidence and trust in Vickie grew, the boss gave up his my-way-or-the-highway approach and gradually gave her more and more responsibility. She delivered the goods and made sure the boss got most of the credit.

Interestingly, Vickie had a colleague, Janet, who also felt that the leader's decisions were seriously flawed. But instead of adopting Vickie's slowly-but-surely and make-him-look-good strategy, she flat out refused to follow orders, insisting that she knew the business better. Janet didn't last two weeks in the new regime. Vickie, on the other hand, played her cards just right. Her responsibilities grew and she enjoyed a steady stream of raises, promotions, and bonuses.

Salute the Rank

We can't emphasize enough how important it is to salute the rank—in other words, to respect the boss's *position* regardless of whether you even like or respect the person.

It's entirely possible that your boss is, in your opinion, a complete buffoon who should really be working in the mailroom. But guess what: That's not your decision. The boss was hired by people who trust him and believe in him, and it's not up to you to show them they were wrong. In fact, trying to do so will come back to blindside you faster than you think.

(Continued)

> Your overriding objective is to protect yourself. And the best way to do that is to make everyone think that your boss is God's gift to business. Making him look good, giving him credit for your great ideas, and supporting him every chance you get, means that he will trust you. And the more he trusts you, the more likely he will give you added responsibilities and bring you into his inner circle. Eventually, when you really need it, he will put his weight behind you and support *you* as you make a career move in the company.
>
> Ultimately it comes down to this: Making your boss look good works for you in countless ways. This strategy actually puts you in charge and, most importantly, it enhances your reputation within the company.

Exceed Expectations

Another very effective way of managing your boss is to exceed her expectations. Now don't be concerned: This isn't going to create a conflict with "don't outshine the master," because if your achievements make your boss look great, she won't see you as a competitor, but as an indispensable member of her team. She'll also get kudos for recognizing your talents and keeping you on board.

In many cases it's possible—and wise—to combine "Make the boss look good" and "Exceed expectations." Michelle Tazor, director of benefits at a large Chicago hospital, had a situation where she had to do exactly that. Michelle had been with the company for several years before her new boss—the first woman president of the hospital—came on board. Almost immediately, Michelle noticed a pattern: Ten minutes before every hospital board meeting, Michelle would get a frantic phone call from her boss asking for the latest staffing numbers.

Michelle, a classic, everything in-its-place, results-focused manager, quickly realized that her new boss, despite being a captivating speaker and a dynamic presenter, wasn't a detail person. She wasn't sufficiently prepping for her meetings and didn't take enough time to properly vet her materials. Although she gave an enthusiastic report, her constantly searching for numbers made her appear unprepared and ineffective in front of the board.

Michelle realized that the smartest thing she could do to make her boss look good was to ensure that her boss had the latest headcounts and most accurate stats on benefits—well before each board meeting. Michelle asked her boss's assistant to alert her whenever a board meeting was scheduled so that she could ask her boss to block out some time to meet and rehearse the numbers.

Michelle's efforts paid off. Taking it upon herself to help prepare her boss more thoroughly before board meetings ensured that the boss succeeded in front of the board. It also increased Michelle's visibility and access. She came up with a way to exceed expectations, and it certainly increased her chances for advancement.

Bring Solutions, Not Problems

It is often said that there are two types of employees: the ones with the can-do attitude and the ones who spend their time running around complaining that the sky is falling. The smartest way to achieve, get promoted, and increase your power base is to be the person your boss looks to *first* when there's something that needs to be done.

Elaine Eisenman had the opportunity to put this rule into action at the start of a new job. One of her first assignments was to organize the company's first-ever, on-site town hall meeting for 300 employees. Plans were made, reviewed, changed, reviewed again, and finally agreed on. Elaine and her team did a masterful job of turning the company cafeteria into a state-of-the-art meeting facility. The evening before the meeting, as Elaine was taking care of the final details, she got a call from her boss, the company chairman, telling her that he had invited 100 more people from the company's distribution center to attend the meeting. The problem was that the cafeteria was already packed to capacity and she couldn't squeeze in 10 more chairs, let alone 100. But she knew that something had to be done.

Elaine immediately went to see her facilities manager, who was still on-site, and told him they needed to set up a second venue in the company parking lot, complete with tenting, 100 chairs, speakers, staging, and video screen. It was apparent that until the change was completed, no one was going home that night. Elaine called her boss and told him she had found a solution and would see him first thing in the morning. Everything went off without a hitch.

The bring-me-solutions mandate is never actually written or spoken out loud. But if you practice it, you are taking significant steps toward securing your power base.

Protect Your Boss's Back

Protecting your boss's back is a fairly straightforward rule. First, keep confidential any professional or personal issues that might reflect negatively on your boss. Second, stand in for your boss, without hesitation, if ever he is unavailable—but as always, be sure to give him credit. And third, never use your position to trade insider information. The more your boss relies on you to cover his back, the more he'll protect you in return. For a boss, there is nothing more reassuring than a trusted subordinate who walks into the office, closes the door, and says, "Heads up! I just heard that . . ."

Carlos Hernandez-Sims, VP of finance at a large financial services company in Detroit, knew how important it was to protect his boss's back. When his boss, the CFO, was on a well-earned vacation backpacking in Panama, the company suddenly faced a budget crisis. Because Carlos's boss was away, the chairman turned to Carlos for answers. Carlos knew he'd have to come up with some decisive recommendations in a hurry. But he also knew that his vacationing boss would want to review the numbers before anything was given to the chairman.

Of course, reaching someone who's backpacking in the wilderness can be quite a challenge. But working through the trip outfitter who had organized the journey, Carlos was able to set up an emergency satellite phone call to the jungle campsite. He let his boss know that the chairman was demanding numbers asap, and he got approval for what he planned to present to the chairman. The following morning as Carlos gave his report, he made very clear that everything had been prepared in consultation with the CFO, direct from the jungle, the evening before. The chairman was impressed at Carlos's candor and ingenuity, the CFO was grateful to have had someone watching his back, and Carlos's career took a noticeable leap forward. It doesn't get any better than that.

PERCEPTION TRAPS

We have laid out a very clear plan for how to manage up the ranks, but there's one thing that can really throw you a curve: others' perceptions.

How other people in your company *perceive* the bond between you and your boss is often more important than reality. It doesn't matter what's *really* going on; all that counts is what they *think* is going on—because that's what they're going to tell the guy in the next cubicle, who will e-mail it to a buddy in another department, who will tell his secretary over lunch, and before you know it, one person's completely inaccurate perception can become your reality. Of course that can sometimes work in your favor, but most of the time it's an ambush waiting to happen. For that reason, you absolutely must continually monitor your coworkers' perceptions. Doing so will keep you from falling into the common perception traps that have prematurely ended the careers of a number of talented executives we know. Let's look at the three most common ones:

1. Mini me syndrome
2. Confidante conundrum
3. Transference phenomenon

Mini Me Syndrome

Who wouldn't want to work for a powerful, influential, dynamic leader? All three of us have enjoyed it at one time. Working for this kind of boss can be an extraordinary learning opportunity, giving you a rare occasion to see first-hand how a truly impressive leader motivates, commands, and deliberates. At the same time, a strong manager will push you hard to succeed and in most instances will coach you toward a promotion.

That said, being closely associated with such a powerful and dynamic personality can be risky. If others *perceive* you as being little more than an extension of your boss, a "mini me," you're in danger of losing credibility. Every time you say things like, "When I met with the chairman, he said that we should . . ." or "The president wants . . ." or "The boss and I were thinking . . . ," you create or reinforce the impression that you have no authority or power of your own and that you are not making any independent decisions. Obviously, this kind of negative perception begins to undermine any hopes you have of advancing in your career. So you'll need to think strategically about how to articulate your ideas with a distinct and separate voice.

Here's your game plan: Even if you're going to publicly talk about something your boss created, frame your delivery in a way that doesn't make you sound like the ventriloquist's dummy. Use "I" instead of "we" in your presentations. Be very, very careful not to take credit for something that your boss did. It's okay for her to do that but it's a one-way street. Reserve the "we" for talking about your team.

On an ongoing basis, ask for projects and assignments that you can author or lead on your own. Suggest to your boss that you deliver a portion of one of her presentations. Make your own social connections and stay away from restaurants that your boss frequents.

At this point you may be wondering whether what we're saying here conflicts with everything we said earlier about making your boss look good. It doesn't. Delivering your own presentations and making your own connections strengthens your professional credibility and prevents you from losing your identity.

Confidante Conundrum

Consigliore, Italian for "counselor" or "adviser," is a term most often associated with the Mafia. And if you're familiar with *The Godfather* or *The Sopranos*, you've caught a glimpse of just how exciting and powerful being the don's primary adviser can be. Becoming your boss's confidante can be just as tantalizing. It puts you right at the seat of power. You're privy to all sorts of confidential information, you have an opportunity to meet influential people, and this connection gives you a head start in building up your networks faster than your peers.

However, the problem with being in the shadow of the throne is that others throughout the organization, regardless of their level, will see you as a manager with only *reflected power*, not earned power. For example, if you are the head of strategic planning reporting directly to the CEO, you have the power to tell the business unit presidents, all of whom sit at a much higher level in the company, that they need to meet your deadlines for strategy planning reports. The presidents are neither your peers nor your subordinates and they certainly don't answer to you. They will meet the deadlines because you're acting in your boss's stead, *not* because you gave the order and not because they respect your authority.

Earned power is different, and it's exactly what it sounds like: power you've acquired through your *own* accomplishments. In most cases and in most organizations, managers and executives with bottom-line responsibilities are perceived as having earned power, while those in staff or administrative roles are perceived as having reflected power. It is often not that easy to decipher who has real power. In the next chapter, we look at reflected power in staff positions, power that can be critical to your success.

Just to be clear, reflected power is not always a negative. In fact, sometimes it can be an amazing tool. Reflected power gives you access—which you can use as a kind of ongoing audition—to the people above you in the chain of command. The head of strategic planning we just mentioned, while delivering the CEO's messages, could impress one of the division presidents with his competence and loyalty. Because access is often a key factor to moving your career ahead, reflected glory can be a great thing if you keep it in perspective and use it wisely.

Serving as a consigliore carries yet another downside. Because you have your boss's ear, managers and executives in your organization may see you as their own ticket to the big time. They may flatter you, sweet-talk you, and even come right out and try to sway you with expensive lunches or 50-yard-line football tickets. But look out: As Machiavelli wisely warned, "Flatterers abound because men are so easily pleased with their own qualities and are deceived by them."[2]

There is a real danger here. If you can't assess how much influence you really have, how can you realistically gauge your own talents and abilities? If you aren't getting honest feedback, or you misperceive your power, you run the risk of being blindsided. The smartest way to minimize the risk and deal with this conundrum is to limit the amount of time you stay on as a consigliore.

We know first-hand that it's hard to give up the perks and the flattery. But even though you might not want to part with your key to the executive washroom, you'll eventually damage your career and your reputation if you stay too long. Knowing how to recognize the external signs that it's time to move on are important. Here are three things you should pay attention to:

1. *The calendar.* Don't stay in the consigliore position for any longer than three years. In your first year, you're getting your feet firmly planted and building trust with the boss. In the second year, hopefully, you're learning from a master and reaping the rewards of the proximity to the corner office. In year three, you should be making sure your exit strategy is current and ready to go.
2. *Search firms.* When you start getting more calls from headhunters looking for referrals than trying to lure you away, it's time to update your resume. There may be a perception in the market that you are comfortable and in for the long term.
3. *Peer promotions.* When a colleague of parallel rank is promoted over you, there may be a perception in the company that you are attached to a powerful boss and not looking to move away.

Although execs of both genders can have trouble recognizing when it's time to make a change, it's especially difficult for women. They often become too comfortable in the confidante role, too eager to keep the access, and misjudge how they're perceived. To avoid an I-didn't-see-it-coming moment, women should be sure to place strict limits on the amount of time they serve as confidantes and always be on the lookout for opportunities to shine on their own merits.

Transference Phenomenon

How many times have you heard someone in a work situation say, "You remind me of . . ." As flattering as that may sound, it could be a major trap, because once you trigger an association with another person, you have no control over how your actions or performance will be perceived or interpreted.

The problem is what psychoanalysts call *transference*, a term that describes the common phenomenon of patients who drag behavior patterns and emotions out of their past and overlay them onto their therapist. These patients can't separate out previous experiences from current ones.

What does this have to do with you and your job? Plenty, according to Manfred F.R. Kets de Vries and Michael Maccoby, a pair of psychologists who have applied transference theory to organizational settings. Both found extensive examples of transference having significant impact on relationships between bosses and their direct reports.[3] If you think about it, it makes sense. For example, hearing someone speak with a southern drawl probably brings up different images of the speaker in your mind than if the same words were spoken with an upper-class British accent.

Because transference is an unconscious process, it can be extremely difficult to identify. When it does kick in, however, it can have an impact on your career. Consider it a possible explanation for reactions that leave you shaking your head and don't seem to make sense.

Transference may be affecting your career if you've ever heard your boss tell you:

- You sound like his overbearing mother.
- You remind her of a high school rival.

- You remind him of his favored son or delinquent daughter.
- You dress like her ex-husband.
- You laugh like his beloved grandfather.
- You argue like his ex-wife.
- You criticize like her first boss.
- You remind him of his high school girlfriend.

When Winnie Jacobs was promoted to general manager at a large Midwest television station, she happily inherited a crackerjack, top-notch sales team. Two months into the job, though, her director of sales was promoted to run a station in another nearby city, leaving an unexpected opening on her team. Everyone else on the team felt that Tony Scarlotto, who had been the top-performing sales exec for the past three years running, was a shoo-in for the job. But to everyone's amazement, Winnie started interviewing candidates and Tony couldn't even get in to make a pitch.

One evening, at a preview screening of the next season's programming, Tony happened to sit next to a company VP in from out of town, who looked at him, did a double take, and said, "Did anyone ever tell you that you look exactly like Winnie Jacobs' ex-husband? Whew, that was one nasty divorce." Tony had his answer and the next morning he cracked open his Rolodex and started making calls to headhunters.

Unfortunately, memories—especially negative ones—are extremely difficult to dislodge. How can you successfully manage your boss when you trigger a knee-jerk response just by walking into his office? His reaction has nothing to do with *you*, of course, but short of major surgery, no amount of recasting will change his perception.

We don't think, however, you should just throw in the towel and walk out the door immediately. See if you can get some insight into what's triggering the negative reaction. Another option is to just hang in for a while and do your job unbelievably well to see if you can get past it. But if the friction continues, then it's time to activate your exit strategy.

CHAPTER 7   Takeaways

1. Never outshine the master.
2. Be your boss's biggest fan, inside and outside the organization.
3. Exceed expectations and become an indispensable member of the team.
4. Be a can-do employee.
5. Protect your boss's back.
6. Never serve in a confidante role for more than three years.
7. Manage perceptions artfully so you're not seen as a "mini me."
8. Remember that transference can be the explanation for reactions that do not make sense.

8

HIDDEN INFLUENTS, OR THE ART OF MANAGING CORPORATE STAFF

Almost every company has an organization chart—you know, all those little boxes connected by lines—that supposedly illustrates the flow of power within the company. Well, org charts are fine and dandy, but they don't do a very good job of explaining how power *really* flows. A far more accurate chart would look like a map of rivers and influents or tributaries. A large number of tiny creeks or employees flow into a lesser number of brooks or supervisors, which flow into a still smaller number of streams or managers, until a handful of major waterways or senior management empty into the sea—or into the C-suite.

Unfortunately, even a map of influents has its shortcomings: What you can't see there—and what you can't see in your company—are all the currents that flow just below the surface. But make no mistake: Just because you can't see these powerful eddies, doesn't mean they don't pose a risk. These hidden influents are known in organizations as "staff"—managers in finance, HR, and legal—and one smart way of winning in a company is to learn how to successfully manage them.

Why are these influents important to you? The simplest answer is that they have *access*—usually a straight shot to senior management, and sometimes directly to the CEO. What you should keep in mind is that they can use their power to influence how management evaluates and perceives you.

They also have insider *knowledge* and use it to wield power that, on the surface, they do not seem to need, court, or desire. But don't be fooled by this impression. It's critical that you not only understand their power, but befriend, respect, and align yourself with them as well. Having strong ties to the organization's influents could help you get out of sticky situations and even clear some of the obstacles off of your road to the top. Conversely, ignoring these people or misjudging their power will bog you down, create roadblocks, or worse, get you blindsided!

Before we go on, let's talk about one other group of even less apparent influents: consultants. They may not be staff, but they're *paid invited guests* and they often have the support and backing of some very powerful executives. Generally speaking, consultants are professional advisers, brought in from outside by management to handle a reorganization, manage special projects, realign staff, or even help downsize a company.

What does this have to do with you? Plenty. These rogue influents often roam freely inside the company, and provide an organizational report card to the president or other top management. Consultants have the ear of the powerful and are masters of the pointed whisper. That puts them in position to sing your praises or dash your hopes. Smart managers should never diss hidden influents or consultants. You need to align with them effectively throughout your career and develop what Michael Watkins, in his book *The First 90 Days*, calls "relationship capital," so you can leverage their influence to your best advantage.[1]

FINANCIAL JUGGERNAUT

The CFO is the most powerful influent in the organization. He signs off on all significant compensation packages, internal budgets, relocation costs, and real estate leases, and interprets the earnings for the press. He has a wide sphere of influence and will be involved in areas that affect every operating manager, including promotions, raises, bonuses, and dismissals. The CFO is the guy with all the answers; his report on the financials is the centerpiece of every board of directors meeting. The CEO won't talk to Wall Street without the CFO at his side. Unfortunately for the CFO, sharing the glory sometimes means sharing the blame. We saw that in the Enron, WorldCom, and HealthSouth debacles, where the CFOs and CEOs shared the front-page headlines and some have ended up with adjoining cells.

Because the CFO is the financial juggernaut or bastion of power, you can't afford not to have her in your corner. And the best way to get her there is to learn her language: numbers. How? No matter what you ask for, such as adding staff or request for capital improvement, make sure you can demonstrate the return on investment or ROI. If the CFO and her direct reports are on board with you, they'll be able to make a strong case on your behalf with even higher layers of management. And while you're at it, remember that sometimes you may need to justify *yourself* to the CFO. If the CFO doesn't feel that you're making a substantial contribution to the bottom line of the company, she can be lethal to you; all it takes is a few well-chosen negative words to senior management. It goes beyond "no support, no projects." If you're not on your game all the time, you can easily get sandbagged.

Mary Ahern learned this lesson the hard way. She was in her first month of a newly created position as chief marketing officer at Midfield Sports, a regional retail sports equipment chain with more than 500 stores. Until Mary was hired, marketing had always been part of the store design department. Encouraged by the board to bring in a marketing guru to help expand the customer base, the CEO hired Mary. But the CFO and a handful of other senior executives were skeptical. They pointed to the company's sustained rapid growth without a marketing star, and concluded that Mary was a very expensive—and completely unnecessary—addition. The CFO wanted proof that she would add to the bottom line.

Mary's first initiative was to create a direct-mail campaign centered on point-of-purchase redemption coupons. She planned to present results of the campaign three weeks after coupon expiration. At that time, they would be four months into the project and full results could be analyzed. Much to Mary's surprise, just one month after launch, at the regularly scheduled Monday morning staff meeting, the CFO grilled Mary about the new campaign and asked for redemption-to-date sales information. Unprepared for this question, she attempted to tap dance, explaining why it was too early for any meaningful reports. Without preliminary numbers at her fingertips, Mary came across as defensive and uncertain about the progress of the campaign. Her credibility was seriously damaged. And to make matters worse, the CEO ordered Mary to have the numbers on his desk by the end of the day.

Mary had stepped on quite a few landmines. Because she was new to the company and launching a unique campaign, she never should have assumed that the CFO would wait a whole month to get numbers. Every executive must always be prepared for pop quizzes at any time. Mary had also forgotten how important it is to have relationship capital, particularly with such a powerful influent. The CFO was already gunning for her, and her failure to follow the Boy Scout motto, "Be prepared," allowed him to launch an attack that essentially confirmed he had been right to question her hire. Mary also put herself in a vulnerable position by not following the cardinal rule: Never go into a staff meeting without your numbers! She should have seen it coming.

What could Mary have done differently? To start with, she could have skillfully co-opted the CFO by giving him advance information on her campaign, making him feel like a comrade. She could also have garnered his support by explaining why she needed three months to deliver the goods and create gains for the company. She missed what we call the *inside sell*—the support you rally within the company to form a core team of believers. It's critical to take these steps with all hidden influents, not just line managers. Think of it as an internal public relations campaign.

Let's take a look at a situation where someone successfully leveraged the CFO's support. Ellen Konoko was a newly hired senior VP of marketing for KidCo, a children's toy retailer in Minneapolis. The CFO, Harriet Lind, approved a department budget that was too small and unrealistic for the marketing campaign Ellen had designed. Boldly, Ellen countered the numbers by suggesting that Harriet reallocate money from the operations side of the business, which was focused on new store openings, so that her marketing could be more aggressive. Harriet listened, but explained that the operations side had no fat since new stores were being opened quarterly and the openings were already over budget.

Since Ellen had no recourse but to accept what she saw as insufficient funds, she did so calmly. But that didn't keep her from thinking about how to give Harriet a reason to reallocate money in her favor. Ellen hired a small outside marketing team within the confines of her budget and focused on scoring an immediate win with a pilot project. Once the pilot worked, Ellen drew up a specific business plan showing not only the successful results, but also how these results could be expanded to translate into greater revenue for the company.

Armed with her business plan and pilot project success in hand, Ellen put together an expanded marketing budget to cover new campaigns and presented it to Harriet *before* taking it to anyone else in the organization. Harriet was impressed, not only with Ellen's initiative, but also with having the opportunity to review the plan before it went to the CEO. Flattered to have been brought into the tent, Harriet approved the additional funds for marketing. This was a real hat trick for Ellen. Marketing ended up with an expanded budget, Ellen's profile in the company soared, and she now had a very powerful ally in her corner.

BODIES, BENEFITS, AND BOUNDARIES

Of all the staff functions inside the organization, the human resources department holds the deepest secrets of the company. Although the HR staff can't reveal most of what they know, they have their pulse on the inner wiring of the organization. People often view HR as a bureaucratic iceberg that gets in the way of the business flow. In many ways they're right. And that's because it's designed that way. Human resources no longer simply supervises the hiring function or acts as the corporation's police force. In the twenty-first century, HR, along with the legal department, is charged with insuring that the organization protects itself from lawsuits by making sure everyone dots the i's and crosses the t's. As the core service arm of the organization, HR also has the responsibility to be the standard-bearer of the company's values. In some companies, the senior VP of HR actually has an office in the C-suite.

Unfortunately, most managers and executives underestimate HR's influence and power. But because HR has the capability to help you with hiring, firing, reference checking, training, company history, and former and current procedures, one of the smartest things you can do is go out of your way to forge friendships and alliances with the men and women who work there. If you know how to leverage their resources, HR can be a tremendous support to you at every stage of your climb inside the company.

But watch out. If you cross them, HR staff can stop you in your tracks. If, for example, you get so frustrated by bureaucratic paperwork and wheel-spinning that you try to circumvent HR procedures, you might as well hang a "blindside me" sign on your back. Take the example of Bob Noyes. Bob was director of the East Coast distribution center for Cobblestone Farms, a fast-growing distributor of organic foods based in New Hampshire. At the core of Cobblestone Farms' image was their well-known value statement: "Always committed to serving our customers with the highest integrity." To keep up with expanding national distribution demands, the board decided to build a second distribution center, this one on the West Coast. Bob would then be promoted to vice president of national distribution and assume responsibility for both centers. But here's the kicker: Bob's promotion wouldn't take effect until he had hired a new director to head each center. Until then, he'd have to continue in his current job, dividing his time and directing both centers.

Noyes worked directly with Betsy Blaine, vice president of HR, to create a job description for both positions and to bring on a search firm to find candidates. Sooner than anyone expected, they hired Stephen Link as director for the East Coast distribution center. Link then recommended a former colleague, Phil Carsen, for the West Coast position. Noyes was delighted that the process was moving so quickly and met Carsen the following week. Everyone at the company liked Carsen, and Noyes wanted to make him an immediate offer. But Betsy Blaine insisted that the standard hiring practices be followed and asked the search firm to check references.

A couple of days later, Blaine received an anonymous call in her office: "Phil Carsen is bad news." Blaine, duly alerted, called the search firm to see what they had found in their reference checking. The reports were decidedly mixed: No one was saying anything negative about Carsen, but they couldn't find anyone who was fully positive either. Blaine delivered the news to Noyes and expressed her concern about bringing Carsen on board. Noyes discounted the information and claimed that the anonymous caller was probably a disgruntled former employee. Blaine suggested that she and Noyes discuss this with his friend Link since he had made the recommendation. Sheepishly, Link admitted that there had been some minor issues in Carsen's past—he'd been accused of sexual harassment—but since nothing was ever proven, Link felt that there was nothing there.

The search firm confirmed the harassment charge, but was less certain that all had been resolved. Learning this, Blaine told Noyes that she would not support hiring Carsen without a more thorough investigation. Noyes argued. He was impressed with Carsen's credentials and expertise, and he needed him *now*! So he tried pressuring Blaine to make the offer.

Backed into a corner, Blaine had to make a decision. She decided that even if Carsen were innocent of the charges, the values and public persona of Cobblestone Farms were being threatened. So she went directly to the company's CEO, who backed Blaine. The CEO understood Noyes's urgency, but Blaine's logic and concern for the company's image won out. Carsen was not hired. Noyes remained at Cobblestone Farms but the CEO had clearly lost faith in his judgment. Not a good place to be.

Executives who downplay or disregard HR's influence and integrity quotient are treading in dangerous waters. Managers often try to bypass or override HR to fill positions quickly, never paying attention to the protections that HR can provide. Big mistake. Line executives may want to let the end justify the means when it comes to hiring, but HR has a higher calling: protecting the company's legal position, ultimate reputation, and, believe it or not, you.

No matter how frustrated you may feel at having to toe the bureaucratic line, you should still go out of your way to keep an open and cordial dialogue going with HR. The HR staff are like the canaries in the coal mine. A little twitter here, an unusual silence there, and a friendly HR staffer can alert you to upcoming events that might be useful for the team—or for you.

At ABC, Amy Kopelan used to drop in frequently on Bill Wilkinson, head of HR. They developed a long-standing friendship. When Bill's niece needed a summer internship, Amy opened the door in her department. Because of an earned mutual respect, Bill offered Amy important and strategic advice when she negotiated her exit package from ABC.

When Nancy Widmann moved to HR early in her CBS career, she worked side-by-side with Joan Showalter, an exceptional executive who headed compensation in corporate HR, and they became good friends. This alliance continued as both women climbed the CBS executive ladder. Joan became the respected and admired head of HR, and was known affectionately as the "Godmother" of CBS. She shepherded the company through times of turmoil and helped Nancy handle many personnel crises that affected the radio division. Joan was an important and valued ally.

Here's some advice that will keep you on HR's good side. Too many HR professionals have memories like elephants. When a time comes that you need a favor or need to slide past a rule, HR won't be predisposed in your direction unless you have earned their support.

To keep the alliance strong and working to your benefit, *do not*:

- Treat HR staffers like glorified secretaries or gofers.
- Bring in your own search firms without getting HR's approved list first.
- Promise raises and/or promotions to your staff unless you've first cleared them with HR for consistency with others in similar jobs or grades.
- Fail to attend a meeting arranged at your request to discuss a performance problem with a member of your staff.
- Say anything remotely politically incorrect in a public place and then try to explain away your gaffe by saying, "But everyone knew I was kidding."
- Miss the deadlines for performance appraisals, bonus recommendations, merit increases, or job requisitions.
- Yell, "With all the paperwork you require, it's impossible to run a business!"
- Tell HR it's their responsibility to develop job specs for your department's open positions.
- Be out of the office when candidates have been scheduled for job interviews.
- Ask for confidential information about compensation issues.

NEGOTIATORS AND REGULATORS

Imagine you are the CEO. You look to your lawyers to protect the organization's interests and assets at all costs. Sure, they want you to land that $10 million contract you've been working on for the past year. But if it looks to them as though that $10 million contract could expose the company to $20 million in liabilities, the lawyers are going to shut the deal down. This happens in business every day. If you, as a lower-level manager with a complicated deal on the table, have a positive relationship with legal, there is a good chance that they will spend the extra effort to clear the obstacles so you can pull the deal off.

In this era of Sarbanes-Oxley, the SEC, IRS, FDA, and other regulatory bodies, and the endless securities and oversight issues to wade through, corporate attorneys are more influential than ever before, and have direct access to and, in many cases influence over, the CEO, CFO, and other senior managers.[2] Successful executives know when and where to rely on the legal department. When it comes to company assets or reputation, the legal department will have the necessary weapons to fight off an attack or adversary. No matter how powerful you think you are, don't cross them. Don't try to outfox them. Don't think about trying to slip a deal under the radar. Try to go it alone and you'll set yourself up to be blindsided.

The Latham Management Group, headquartered in Edison, New Jersey, has been a leader in the destination management business for over 10 years. Latham is often brought in to design and manage on-site staging and production for large sales meetings and exceptional events, including the Atlanta Olympics, the U.S Tennis Open in Flushing Meadows, and New York Fashion Week. Latham's founder and chairman, Ilene Lefkowitz, employed a top-notch sales force, most of whom had been with the company from the beginning.

Following 2004 Fashion Week, Pauline Palmer, the assistant sales manager for the northeast region, asked to see Bill Ford, an attorney in the legal department with whom she had worked on several client contracts. Palmer had been with the company for almost eight years and was a loyal employee. In a closed-door meeting, Palmer confided to Ford that Latham's senior account executive, Jason Marcus, had tried to recruit her to join him in leaving Latham and starting his own business. He had offered Palmer an equity position in his new company if she would provide him with the proprietary client and vendor information that he couldn't access.

Palmer was upset. She had no intention of leaving with Marcus, nor did she intend to help him. But she was terrified that she might be implicated in his scheme if anyone found out that he had discussed it with her. Bill Ford told her that she was doing the right thing and arranged for her to talk with the general counsel. Palmer met with the general counsel, told her everything, and asked for guidance. The legal department sprang into action. They advised Palmer to stay home and not come into the office the following day.

Twenty minutes later, the general counsel met with Lefkowitz in her office and told her about the situation, highlighting Palmer's courage in coming to them for help. They then planned the next steps, which involved Lefkowitz and the general counsel meeting with Marcus and confronting him about his mutiny. Marcus admitted his plans and the general counsel quietly escorted him out of the building. Pauline Palmer ended up a hero.

Earlier we talked about how dealing with HR can sometimes be slow and frustrating. Unfortunately, the same is often true of your legal department's attorneys. Sometimes it seems as though they're working in molasses. They'll review . . . and review . . . and review, until you're just about ready to chuck the deal papers out the nearest windows, followed immediately by the lawyers. It can seem that they are deliberately holding up negotiations. And all too often, they can get into one-upmanship contests with the other side's lawyers over matters that seem to you to be more about ego than substance. At some point you may find yourself asking whose side the lawyers are on. And the answer may surprise you!

The truth of the matter is that the company's lawyers are *not* on your side. They're on the company's side. That's a subtle but very important distinction. The lawyers' responsibilities are to the organization. People who forget this often find themselves running smack into walls.

Never try to oversell the company lawyer on your deal. Don't overlook or withhold certain facts that she needs to know. It is a surefire way to set yourself up for an explosion. If you are evasive, or if the lawyers feel you are hiding something, rest assured they will slow down your deal, your operation, your progress, and—if it happens often enough—your career. We've seen far too many executives fall prey to their own cleverness.

A Short Course in Getting Your Company's Lawyers on Your Side

- Call them in early and leverage their expertise to your advantage. Whatever it is that you're working on, they've done it a thousand times.
- Never keep them out of things that have legal implications—even small things.
- Never create camouflage. Full disclosure is mandatory! So be completely honest when presenting them the deal breakers versus negotiable items, as well as

potential problem areas or pitfalls, or even the slightest weakness in your position.

- Come prepared. Anticipate the questions—especially the ones you don't want to deal with—and have your answers ready.

A Slightly Longer Course to Making Enemies of Your Company's Lawyers

Want the lawyers to mistrust you? Want to get blindsided in a hurry? Here are some things you *never* want to say to your attorneys.

- "I didn't know I was supposed to check with you guys on small stuff like that."
- "The deal would have blown up if I didn't sign the papers, and the contract read just like the last one."
- "I'll be out of pocket until the end of the week on a really important deal; you won't be able to reach me."
- "Senior management really wants this to work. I don't see what the problem is."
- "It's too late to make any changes now; it's at the printers."
- "We can't touch this guy. He's our biggest producer. Can't you find some other way?"
- "We're ramping up so I can't make that meeting."
- "To be perfectly honest with you . . ."
- "There's always room for interpretation."

ROGUE INFLUENTS

Some of the most frightening words an executive can ever hear come out of the mouths of consultants who show up bright and early Monday morning and announce, "I'm here to help." Consultants brought in by senior management rarely have clearly enunciated roles and objectives—at least not that they're willing to share with you. No small wonder that it's hard to figure out their true agenda. Because consultants brought in by senior management rarely arrive with a purpose or agenda you can quantify, we think of consultants as rogue influents. Why? *Rogue* signifies unpredictable, operating outside normal controls—a pretty apt description for these guns for hire.

Some argue that consultants serve a strategic and well-intentioned purpose. That's definitely so—sometimes. In times of crisis, a consultant may bring just the right knowledge or make the exact recommendation that's needed to keep a company alive. Consider the crisis management consultant who helped Air Florida talk to the press when there was the crash over the Potomac, or the consultants who helped Johnson & Johnson during the Tylenol recall. Consultants can prove to be positive influents on an organization. They are particularly adept at helping companies plan out cultural transformations. Managers located within the corporate core find it hard to reshuffle divisions and change the environment. In these situations, a consultant's freedom as an outsider permits him to ask questions that no insider would dare to ask.

But too often, rogue influents live up to their name, hiding behind supposed objectivity, ready to blindside you. First, a story.

When Elaine Eisenman was a senior HR executive, she was assigned to oversee a team of consultants the CEO brought in to reengineer the processes in accounting and other financial services and assess the operations of the finance department as a whole. The CEO and the board had some serious concerns about whether the CFO was effectively leading his department, and they thought that objective experts would be able to answer the question.

When their very expensive project was finished, the consultants submitted a report to Elaine with an analysis that completely sidestepped leadership issues. Elaine challenged the consultants about their findings. Although she certainly wasn't mandating criticism of the CFO if it weren't warranted, she thought the CEO had been clear in the assignment's objectives, which included a complete review of the company's financial processes, from the top down. But the consultants' report didn't include a single mention of the CFO or his office.

After some lame rationalizations, the lead consultant pointed out to Elaine that since the CFO was the one signing off on the bill, her team didn't feel comfortable criticizing him. Elaine was floored. She suggested that the consultant look carefully at the name printed on the upper left corner of her last retainer check. It was the company name, not the name of the CFO. Elaine made it clear that until the CFO started writing personal checks to pay for consulting, she expected an objective report. A week or so later, a new report arrived. To no one's surprise, it was highly critical of the CFO's leadership and role within the company. With this analysis in hand, the CEO and the board forced the CFO out. Elaine was alert to the consultants' hidden agenda. Had she accepted a truncated report, her job, not the CFO's, would have eventually been on the line.

Forewarned is forearmed. You need to be particularly on the alert when your boss is the one bringing in a consultant. Clearly, she wants something changed. The land mines here can be as serious as an elimination of a total department or the sale of a division, or as simple as re-alignment of assembly line procedures.

Overall, there are three types of consultants:

1. *"Keep the boss satisfied so we can get more contracts."* These are the guys who, as in Elaine's situation, are more concerned with pleasing the person they perceive to be the moneyman than with producing objective, actionable results.

2. *"Look what a genius I am."* This is the expert who comes in to show upper management how inept the employees are. This consultant performs extensive reviews and inevitably finds something that your team may have identified months ago. For example, your staff may have been pressuring you for months to expand your sales force or for more money for promotional activities. You haven't been able to get management to listen, but now, all of a sudden, it's a great idea!

3. *The carnival barker.* These are the guys who come into the organization making all sorts of unrealistic promises to the person who hired them. They clam they can save the company lots of time, money, and effort, and those promises get repeated and expanded as they work their way through the organization. Rarely, though, do they deliver. The danger to you is that you can fall prey to promises they've made to higher-ups. If a consultant claims that he's going to fix your company's financial woes and make you taller and more beautiful in the next 60 days, be ready to do some reality testing. Try to identify the holes, caveats, and flaws in the proposal so you can defend yourself

and your team. Nothing is worse than having the consultants say the plan was perfect but it fell on its face because you didn't execute properly.

Here's the good news. You can learn to read the true agenda of a consultant who shows up on your doorstep. Let's say your immediate boss calls you to her office to introduce you to a consultant who is coming into the company, or maybe she appears in your doorway with the consultant trailing right behind. Expecting the consultant to disclose the true reason for his appearance is naïve. It's up to you to decode the signals so you can keep from getting blindsided. The process starts by asking the following questions.

- Does the CEO want to combine the operations of several departments or divisions?
- Is there a need to eliminate staff?
- Does the company want to cut costs?
- Do operations need to be outsourced?
- Does the company require new sales incentives?
- Is there a merger possibility?
- Is there a talent audit under way?
- What are the Wall Street analysts saying?
- What are the industry trade journals writing about the company?
- Is someone trying to put "lipstick on the pig" as a first step in the sale of the company?

Once you've asked and answered these questions, you'll be smarter about consultant agendas and, consequently, a lot wiser about how to deal with this paid invited guest.

KNOW WHO YOUR FRIENDS ARE—AND AREN'T

Of all the pitfalls inherent in dealing with consultants, by far the biggest is to make the consultant your friend. Cooperation, mutual respect, and understanding are one thing. Friendship is quite another. In fact, forming a close relationship with a consultant can have dreadful consequences.

Joe Suarez was the senior VP of human resources for a major city newspaper. His boss and publisher, Ed Johnson, asked him to work with a consultant to assess and build the executive team's bench strength. Over the course of a number of months, the consultant became part of the fabric of the company, assessing the current staff and giving feedback on prospective new hires before the offers went out. Joe and the consultant spent increasing amounts of time together, and Joe came to treat the consultant as a friend and confidante.

Six months into the consulting contract, the union threatened a brutal strike, and Ed Johnson worried that the executive team might buckle under pressure. He met with the consultant—without Joe's knowledge—to assess whether the key team members would be able to handle the stress and lead during the upcoming strike. When it came to Joe Suarez, the consultant raised concerns about Joe's resilience and questioned his ability to perform under stress. Joe was a great peacetime leader, he said, but he had no stomach for confrontation.

The assessment confirmed the publisher's fears, but just to be sure, he asked a few other senior execs what they thought. Everyone held Joe in high regard, but no one felt they could trust him to be out front leading the charge when the time came to put on their flak jackets and confront the union.

Johnson was reluctant to tell Joe that he wouldn't be part of the team going forward, but he felt he had no choice. He went into Joe's office to terminate him and used the consultant's report as the primary reason for dismissal. When Joe ran into the consultant in the hall, he looked at him with a bewildered expression and said, "But I trusted you. You were my friend." To make matters worse, in the days that followed, the consultant scored Joe's job.

The moral of the story? Joe made a mistake that many managers do when they deal with a consultant. He misread the relationship. The consultant had been brought into the company by the publisher to prepare for a difficult situation. He sold the publisher on his talent to get the operation ready for a potential strike. He used Joe to gather detailed information on his staff. Joe was in a tough situation and he began to rely on and confide in the consultant. A consultant should never become your ally; he's a gun for hire, and even if you end up with a good working relationship, never let it go further than that.

We have seen too many consultants take down colleagues, either by intent, mishap, or ignorance. Fortunately, if you're prepared, you'll be able to see it coming. Here are our die-hard dozen rules for surviving consultants:

1. Find out who is paying the bills.
2. Always talk to the consultant directly, never through a third party.
3. Initially greet the consultant with enthusiasm.

4. Appear to cooperate at all times, and never lose patience, no matter what the consultant throws at you.
5. Never admit weakness or worries about the strength of members of your team.
6. Share only as much information as you absolutely have to.
7. Make sure your staff is prepped and ready, not nervous and anxious. And instruct them to follow steps 3, 4, 5, and 6 above.
8. Don't automatically dismiss solid advice from the consultant.
9. Don't give away your great ideas.
10. As early in the game as possible, ask to see preliminary findings.
11. Stay actively on top of the process every step of the way.
12. Manage them; don't let them manage you.

To sum it all up, it's critical to your survival that you learn to manage the hidden influents within your organization, whether they are staff or outside consultants. Do whatever you can to make their jobs as easy as possible. View those who have the ear of the powerful as members of your team, not as your adversaries. They just might show you a safer path through the very policies they create and enforce. It can be frustrating at times when you are trying to make your budget, but think of them as giving their expertise instead of trying your patience.

Ultimately, how you manage all the powerful influents in your organization comes down to numbers. Not just the ones on the balance sheet, but also the numbers of people who support you and become part of your power base. The wider that base, both with line and staff, the better off you'll be. Continually work to create allies at all levels of the company; you can be sure a time will come when you'll see a return on those investments in relationship capital.

CHAPTER 8   Takeaways

1. Hidden influents are the secret sources of power inside a company.
2. With a direct line to the top, senior staff can affect how senior management perceives you.
3. Always find ways to keep the CFO firmly in your corner.
4. Never go into a meeting without your numbers, and be prepared for pop quizzes.
5. Build a strong respectful alliance with HR.
6. Never try to sell a deal to the company lawyers.
7. Determine who is setting the agenda and signing the checks for consultants.
8. Treat consultants as paid invited guests, *not* as friends.

9

THE
I-DIDN'T-SEE-IT-COMING MOMENT

We wrote this book with one thing in mind: to help you avoid being blindsided in business. Over the previous eight chapters, we've discussed dozens of situations where your job and/or your career could be derailed. We've shown you how to recognize trouble ahead and what to do to keep potential fallout to a minimum. In this concluding chapter, we give you a fail-safe game plan that will help you hold your head high and maintain a strong sense of control on the day the pink slip hits. And we propose four laws that will help you navigate *any* business minefield.

TEN RED FLAGS AND WHAT THEY MEAN

The Red Flag	*What It Really Means*
1. A coach is brought in to "help" you with conflict resolution.	Management is building a case.
2. You are handed unattainable profit goals.	Management is squeezing you out.
3. You are reassigned from sales to operations	You've been taken off the fast track.
4. Your boss will no longer approve any capital expenditures.	You've lost power.
5. You are not invited to the annual conference.	Management has no future plans for you.
6. There are suddenly many closed-door meetings that you were not informed about.	You are no longer in the information loop.
7. Unfamiliar attorneys are noticed on the executive floor.	Your company is buying or selling.
8. Pressure on you for short-term profits becomes extreme.	The company is being pumped up for a sale.
9. Former adversaries inside the company are seen taking a meeting.	There's a management shift in the wind.
10. Invitations from industry colleagues change from "Let's have dinner" to "How about a cup of coffee?"	Colleagues have heard that you've lost power and are no longer worth the price of a steak.

TEN RED FLAGS AND WHAT THEY REALLY MEAN

We've done literally hundreds of formal and informal surveys and interviews with managers at every level of business. In the course of doing this research, we identified 10 red flags, clear indications that a major change is on the horizon and that getting blindsided is a real possibility. Some of these flags—such as an impending merger or sale—are flapping so wildly in the breeze that they're hard to miss. Some wave more gently and are harder to read, while others barely rustle at all and, unless you're able to put them together with other flags, you might never be aware of problems that are lurking just below the surface.

Of course, not every red flag means that you're perched on the edge of unemployment. But they're usually a strong indication that your career may have just headed down a road you weren't planning to take. The preceding table lists the 10 red flags and what they *really* mean.

To give you an idea of how easily these signs can be missed, we want to tell you a couple of true stories that happened to two well-known executives who, despite all the business savvy in the world, got totally blindsided. (At their request, we have changed their names and companies.) Both of these execs are now in new jobs, happily re-situated. But their lives could have been a lot easier if they'd known what *you* know, having read this book.

Blindsided: "Meet Your New Coach"

Consider the story of Alice Sabatini, a sales manager for a major consumer products company. Alice found herself, almost daily, in the position of having to defend her group to her boss, Moira Sullivan. Even though Alice exceeded her numbers every quarter, her boss constantly challenged her and cut her off in meetings. Alice's and Moira's personalities were very different, and their styles constantly clashed. Alice preferred to present information elaborated with details, stories, and long-winded explanations. Since Moira was a linear thinker, very analytical, and interested in bottom-line results, she was losing patience with her sales manager's rambling style. In other words, the results were great, but the journey to get there was too long. Further, Moira was very uncomfortable with Alice's access to the company's president, who had brought her in from a competitor with great expectations several months earlier.

After five months of difficult interactions, Moira brought in a coach to work with Alice on what she called her "presentation challenges." Moira suggested that having a coach on board would help avoid the daily verbal collisions. Alice agreed, and embraced the opportunity to have a personal coach and sounding board. The coach gave Alice three areas to focus on and Moira signed off on the program. Alice met with the coach weekly and was confident that the issues with her boss were improving. Four months later, without any discussion, Moira fired Alice, claiming that Alice, despite all the coaching, hadn't improved enough to keep her job.

Could Alice have seen it coming? Yes and no. Bringing in a coach to solve someone's personality problems is often a signal that management is planning to fire that person, and has only hired the coach as a way of justifying to HR that management has done its best. On the other hand, bringing in a coach to assist in fast-track development or to build business skills—such as leadership, delegation, and teamwork—shows that management is confident in an executive's potential. You won't be blindsided if you recognize how to spot the difference.

Blindsided: "I'll Look Out for You"

Lewis Bernstein was a senior executive in the career management industry. He'd served as senior vice president for 11 years and had been the number two salesperson in the company's northeast region for three years. The CEO announced that the company was in the process of being bought by one of their largest competitors. This didn't concern Lewis because he had a strong reputation in the business and an impressive list of clients. The CEO planned to remain with the combined organization and needed a trusted lieutenant to interface operations with the acquiring company. He asked Lewis to move out of sales and into operations. The CEO assured him that this was a temporary move, and that he would look out for him as the new management coalesced.

Three months later, deal done, the management slate for the new company was announced. It included five executive vice presidents, but Lewis wasn't on the list. He immediately went to see the CEO to ask for his former line job back. The CEO told Lewis that while he appreciated his hard work in managing the transition, the power to move or promote personnel was out of his hands.

What red flags did Lewis miss? First, when companies are in play, power invariably shifts, and the acquiring company usually has the upper hand. Any assurances made to you (i.e., "I'll look out for you") should be taken cautiously. Second, when Lewis agreed to slide over from sales to operations, he gave up core visibility and sidelined himself.

Finally, Lewis misjudged the loyalty factor. He wrongly assumed that his help with the transition team, combined with 11 years of solid performance, would make him a shoo-in for a new senior position. Instead, he should have started updating his exit strategy the moment he heard the company was changing hands.

WIELDING YOUR POWER ON THE DAY OF RECKONING

No matter how much you've prepared yourself, the day the pink slip arrives is an extremely stressful one. While there's no question that the day of reckoning won't rank as one of the best of your life, don't give in to the temptation to quietly slip out the back door. Initially, of course, you'll steady yourself by focusing on a whole slew of details, such as whom to call, what to say, how to handle your reputation inside and outside of the organization, and what your options are. Those are all logical things to be concerned with. But remember this: You actually hold a great deal of power at this very moment—far more than you'd imagine—and you have a number of options.

So where do that power and those options come from? Consider this: Your employer is concerned. Management wants you to leave quickly and quietly, because your continued presence could cause morale issues within your department and, possibly, the entire company. Word travels quickly. Loyalists on your team could all of a sudden question their own position in the company and wonder whether their heads will be the next to roll. When that happens, anxiety levels go up, while productivity and morale go down.

The company also has to consider the industry as a whole. In this media-driven world, image is paramount, and no one wants negative press. The more senior you are, the more interested the media and Wall Street analysts will be in why you're leaving. What you say as you head out the door may have significant financial implications for your soon-to-be-former employer. In addition, if you're a line manager, the company probably has some serious—and completely justifiable—concerns about how your departure could affect clients, customers, and ultimately the bottom line.

Clearly, the company is depending on your smooth and swift departure. And that puts you in the perfect position to leverage their trepidation and *negotiate the deal you want*. In a sense, they've got you exactly where you want them. Whether you're working as a first-level manager or in the C-suite, you hold the power to negotiate. Don't give up this power. If you have a corporate prenup in place, the terms of disengagement are in writing, but if not, you still have the opportunity to flex your muscles. Don't cave! Your company may not hand over everything you ask for, but that shouldn't stop you from going for as much as you possibly can.

Following are some suggestions or enhancements to ask for. Any or all of these will, at the very least, give you more security and a sense of control over a very difficult situation. Although every company is different, we suggest you begin your negotiations with your immediate boss. If you meet with resistance, or don't get any of the results you want, go to HR and continue the discussion. If you took to heart our advice in Chapter 8 on forging strong connections with HR, you'll know exactly whom to talk with. The caveat here is to remain calm, clear, and un-emotional as you make these requests.

- More severance and an extension of your health coverage.
- Outplacement services and the use of an office and secretarial support for at least three months.
- An extension on your exercise date for stock options.
- A consulting contract for the next few months or short-term contract as an adviser on a project.
- If you plan to launch a new venture, ask for the company to be your first client.

Surviving the Day of Reckoning

- *Don't ever agree to give up your chair immediately.* Insist on coming into the office every day while working out your deal.

- *Call a lawyer who specializes in severance agreements.* This is the best money you'll ever spend. Then, *do not sign anything* from your soon-to-be-former employer until your lawyer has reviewed and approved it.

- *Don't be bullied.* Despite what your boss or HR or anyone else tries to tell you, nothing needs to be signed "by the end of the day." In fact, severance agreements are legal documents that must give you a fixed amount of time, which is subject to negotiation, to review the agreement with your lawyer.

- *Never accept the first severance offer.* There's *always* room for negotiation and the company can *always* do better. If you don't have access to an attorney, take it upon yourself to present a counteroffer to the company. What's the worst that can happen? You might even pull it off.

- *Make sure you and your boss agree on the story of your departure.* Insist that you have a chance to address your team or staff *before* anyone else talks to them.

- *Get veto power over your press releases or announcements inside and outside the company.* If none is to be issued, ask that your boss and HR claim you are leaving to explore other opportunities. Period. The less said the better

- *Never assign blame and be sure to avoid gossip.* When asked, simply say that the timing was right for you to leave. Remember, the business world is small and you never know when you'll find yourself sitting across the desk from a former boss or colleague.

- *Keep it together!* It's in your best interest to remain poised and appear confident at all times. Take the time to say goodbye to colleagues. Perception matters.

We like the example set by Brent Noonan, president of the global games division of a Canadian software company. Brent had taken over the unit at a time when it needed a major turnaround, and under his three-year reign, he transformed it into a well-oiled operation. As

Brent prepared budgets for the coming year, he was aware that senior management was looking for ways to increase profits and scale back his division. The chairman promised Brent that he'd stay the course for 12 more months. But just two months later, Brent was called into the chairman's office to meet with him and the head of HR. They delivered the news that senior management, in consultation with the board, had decided to shut down the games business as quickly as possible and lay off most of the staff, including Brent. They had scheduled a staff meeting for the following morning so they could break the story to the press as soon as possible.

Brent responded calmly. He understood what needed to be done first. In order to control the spin and get the true story out, he insisted that he be the one to address his team. Brent returned to his office and immediately phoned the senior members of his staff, asking that they assemble the entire group the next morning.

Within 24 hours of the announcement, management presented Brent with a severance package. He countered with a plan that was double what the company had offered, and laid out a number of compelling reasons why he should stay on in the role of consultant. He explained that he could effectively finish the projects that were still in production and shut down the unit smoothly. Brent didn't get the full package he asked for, but he got a solid increase in the final severance figure, additional benefit add-ons, and an 18-month consultancy.

Brent Noonan didn't see it coming, but he was still savvy enough to handle the day of reckoning with poise and a full understanding of his power. The company wanted the business shut down seamlessly and quickly, and Brent took full advantage. He insisted on addressing his staff before anyone else approached them, and he controlled the messages given to his team and to the press. After consulting with his attorney, he rejected the first severance offer and confidently asked for more. At the end of the day, Brent managed the situation cleverly and turned a career upheaval into a solid plan for his future.

Is it always possible to be as effective as Brent? Maybe not. But we've learned that most people who follow our guidelines end up with far more than they would have, had they taken the first offer. Without question, being able to leave on your own terms is invaluable in so many ways.

THE FOUR LAWS OF SURVIVAL

There are four critical laws that we always discuss with the clients we coach, the students we teach, and the managers who ask us how to prevent I-didn't-see-it-coming moments. We offer them here for you to use as a guideline for making smart business decisions, and to help you avoid being blindsided at any level of your career. All four are in play at all times, but you'll find that one will be more relevant than another at different stages of your career.

Law 1: It's Always about the Money

All companies, whether public or private, for-profit or not-for-profit, exist to bring money in the door. Period. That simple fact affects you directly and indirectly. On the direct side, money impacts your salary, the resources you have to invest in projects, and whether you can afford to hire that superstar new talent. It dictates whether you can stay at better hotels and travel first-class. And it may ulti-mately determine whether the company stays in business or goes into bankruptcy.

If you're selling a product or a service, it's easy to see how you're impacting the bottom line. It's not quite so clear, though, when you're one or two steps removed from actual selling. Your contribution may be technical, cre-ative, or administrative. But in each case, what you do is vital to the financial health of the operation.

Money is the fuel, the lifeline, the energy, the pulse of every company. Once you get used to this idea, you'll be able to see how the flow of money works, who's making it happen, and how you fit into the scheme of the enterprise. You'll understand that the money report card is always present and that every decision is affected by the financial well-being of the company. As the elevator takes you up in the morning and you're thinking about how to manage your staff, how to create that advertisement, how to de-velop a clearer spreadsheet, or how you can help integrate a new hire into your team, keep your eye on the money and never forget how important it is to you, your career, and the success of the company. In our experience, when-ever anyone says, "It's not about the money," they really mean that it's *all* about the money.

Law 2: Get With the Program

In an era of mergers and acquisitions, cost-cutting and re-organizations, it's critically important to know when and how to get with the program. What program? Well, it's re-ally rather straightforward. At various times over the course of your career, and within your company, you may be asked to support or even lead an initiative that you don't buy into. There are going to be times when you know that it just won't work. Sometimes, getting with the program goes with the territory.

As we see it, the real work of leading is handling this situation with candor. Management is expecting you to rally your troops. One of our clients calls this the "suck it up" moment. The time for commentary and feedback has passed. Getting with the program is such a critical part of basic survival that savvy players learn how to leverage change, stay relevant, and always continue to work hard to improve the plan.

Law 3: Perception Matters

Perception matters. It's that simple. It matters because other people's impressions go a long way toward determining whether they see you as an ally or a competitor, a leader or a follower, a team player or a loose cannon. Perceptions determine whether someone trusts you, believes you, or follows your lead.

It's critical that you understand how *your behavior* impacts people's perception of you. If you embrace the idea that behavior impacts perception, you'll be a lot wiser about the kind of signals you're sending and you'll be less likely to be blindsided by others' reactions. Watch for cues. One way to do that is to ask yourself these three questions:

1. Are people reacting to my words in ways that surprise me?
2. If I'm trying to be collaborative, are others willing to work with me?
3. If I take a tough stand, are others standing behind me?

You can answer these questions only if you're paying attention to how others respond to you. This can be a lot easier if you've followed the advice we gave in Chapter 4 and have a trusted colleague who can provide a reality check.

Perception is based entirely on the how, not the what. Your values and your intentions don't matter. It's what others believe that counts. The old admonition about "walking your talk" is critical here.

Law 4: Always Have an Exit Strategy

And so we come full circle. We started this book with a discussion of exit strategies, and because the idea is so important—and so overlooked—we end with the same advice. In today's turbulent marketplace, since no job is forever, every executive needs a smart and tactical plan that gives him control over his career no matter what happens next, a plan for moving to a new position or out the door.

The exit strategy is your safety net and your peace of mind. With a solid strategy in place, you can lead, innovate, and challenge the status quo without worrying that you will be at risk if the powers that be, or a major sea change, dictate your exit. Having an exit strategy makes you stronger and better able to withstand the vicissitudes of today's business environment.

CONCLUSION

In the introduction to this book we wrote that our goal was "to give you the tools you need to step up, charge for-

ward, and reach for the top without getting blindsided."
We hope we've achieved that. At the very least, we know
that having learned to spot red flags wherever they wave
will give you a greater sense of confidence—the kind that
comes with the knowledge that you can be in charge of
your career. That confidence, in turn, will give you the
power to lead more effectively and creatively.

Finally, we leave you with this thought: Remember to
laugh! Crazy things can and do happen in life and on the
job. And having a sense of humor—especially the ability
to laugh at yourself—will make the insanity, the chaos,
and the unpredictability a lot easier to survive. Good luck!

NOTES

Introduction

1. "Landmine Detecting Flowers," article on the World-Changing web site (www.worldchanging.com), January 27, 2004, www.worldchanging.com/archives/000352 (accessed March 18, 2005).

CHAPTER 2   Taking the Reins

1. Daniel Goleman et al., *Primal Leadership: Realizing the Power of Emotional Intelligence* (Boston: Harvard Business School Press, 2002).
2. Paul Hersey, *The Situational Leader* (New York: Pfeffer & Co., 1992).
3. Louis V. Gerstner Jr., *Who Says Elephants Can't Dance? Inside IBM's Historic Turnaround* (New York: Harper Collins, 2002).
4. Edgar H. Schein, *Organizational Culture and Leadership* (San Francisco: Jossey-Bass, 2004).

CHAPTER 4   Comrades, Coalitions, and Competitors

1. Tom Gegax, *Winning in the Game of Life: Self-Coaching Secrets for Success* (New York: Harmony Books, 1999), 212–213.
2. www.Dictionary.com, retrieved October 14, 2006 at http://dictionary.reference.com/browse/feint.

CHAPTER 5   The Trouble with Teams

1. Friedrich Nietszche, *Beyond Good and Evil*, 1886, Aphorism 156, retrieved October 14, 2006 from Wikiquote at http://en.wikiquote.org/wiki/Friedrich_Nietzsche.
2. Winston Churchill, quoted in James Hunter, *The Wit & Wisdom of Winston Churchill* (New York: Harper-Collins, 1995).
3. Stephen P. Robbins, *The Truth about Managing People . . . and Nothing but the Truth* (Upper Saddle River, NJ: Pearson Education, 2003).
4. Irving L. Janis, *Groupthink: Psychological Studies of Policy Decisions and Fiascoes* (Boston: Houghton Mifflin, 1982).

CHAPTER 6   Surviving a New Boss

1. Robin Hogarth, *Judgement and Choice: The Psychology of Decision* (New York: John Wiley & Sons, 1980), 162.
2. Robert Greene and Joost Elffers, *The 48 Laws of Power* (New York: Penguin Books, 1998), 179.

CHAPTER 7 Managing the Rank above You

1. Robert Greene and Joost Elffers, *The 48 Laws of Power* (New York: Penguin Books, 1998), 1–7.
2. Niccolo Machiavelli, *The Prince* (New York: Bantam Classic, 1981), Letter XXIII, "How Flatterers Must Be Shunned."
3. Manfred Kets de Vries, "Putting Leaders on the Couch: A Conversation with Manfred F.R. de Vries," interview by Diane L. Coutu, *Harvard Business Review* 82, no. 1 (January 2004), 64–71, 113. See also Michael Maccoby, "The Power of Transference," *Harvard Business Review* (September 2004) (reprint R0409E).

CHAPTER 8 Hidden Influents

1. Michael Watkins, *The First 90 Days: Critical Success Strategies for New Leaders at All Levels* (Boston: Harvard Business School Press, 2003), 187.
2. Scott Green, *Sarbanes-Oxley and the Board of Directors* (Hoboken, NJ: John Wiley & Sons, 2005).

INDEX

Index

Index